Morality, Economic Justice, and Profits

Morality, Economic Justice, and Profits

Joseph Webb McLeary

VANTAGE PRESS
New York

Published by Vantage Press, Inc.
516 West 34th Street, New York, New York 10001

Manufactured in the United States of America
ISBN: 0-533-09560-3

Library of Congress Catalog Card No.: 91-90871

0 9 8 7 6 5 4 3 2 1

For Joe, Alan, and Holli

Contents

Acknowledgments

I owe a special word of thanks to my colleagues in the Institute for Executive Leadership at Rhodes College, led by Dr. Larry Lacy and Wayne Pyeatt. The stimulating discussions during those Institute meetings provided the motivation to undertake this book.

Additionally, Dr. Lacy provided continuing encouragement to complete the book at times when business and personal demands seemed to offer ample excuses to delay further efforts to finish. I also appreciate Dr. Lacy's many helpful comments throughout the process of writing and revising the book.

I would like to thank Melinda Reno for all her help in typing and correcting the many drafts of the manuscript.

Introduction

Despite the superior performance of free enterprise economies, there is widespread skepticism about the effect of the profit motive on economic justice and moral behavior. Does the economic system that works best for the most people lack moral justification? Are ethical standards compromised by personal incentives and the profit motive?

Some of those who criticize the ethics of free enterprise defend the justice and morality of a centrally planned system, although these economies have generally performed poorly. More and more countries with controlled economic systems are attempting to improve performance by adopting free market practices. This interesting paradox is readily apparent from the changes now taking place in many countries with state-controlled economic systems.

Although capitalism is clearly superior in providing economic benefits, defending the system in terms of more material goods creates feelings of moral guilt for many people. But superior performance is only part of the morality and economics equation. The moral test of capitalism must take into account both the ethical foundation of the system and the conditions under which the increased benefits are provided.

Throughout this discussion, "profit system," "free enterprise," "market economy," and "capitalism" are used interchangeably. These descriptive expressions are intended as very general contrasts to "socialism," "communism," and "centrally planned economies," although modern capitalism and modern socialism share a number of common features. Modern capitalism emphasizes free market tendencies mixed with social welfare constraints, and modern socialism emphasizes state control mixed with free market characteristics.

References to "morality" and "ethics" refer to standards of right and wrong intentions and conduct of individuals. "Economic justice," on the other hand, refers to the social arrangement of economic affairs that protects the rights of all persons to receive the economic benefits to which they are entitled as human beings. "Economic justice" deals largely with actual results; "morality" also includes the nature of the intentions underlying personal behavior itself. Moral standards, individually and collectively, influence the level of economic justice that is ultimately experienced in an economic system.

Some readers will disagree with the view that economic systems have a separate moral dimension apart from the collective personal behavior of the individuals making up the system. However, the profit system is often criticized for creating lower moral standards of individual behavior. The profits and morality debate is not only about the economic justice of profits and the profit system, it is also about the moral standards of behavior that are influenced by an economic system based on the profit motive. In this sense, the profit system has a moral dimension and is not morally neutral.

The moral objection to capitalism revolves around two issues: (1) a perception that a profit system causes an unjust sharing of economic benefits, and (2) a belief that the system encourages undesirable moral behavior. The system is resented and despised by many, although its benefits are abundant and widespread; in fact, negative attitudes about the profit system are not uncommon on the part of many who clearly share in the general benefits provided by the system. Thus the moral criticism of capitalism is more than just a "sour grapes" argument by the economically deprived.

The purpose of this book is to review the profits and morality debate. No attempt is made to prove the moral superiority of capitalism; rather, the intent is to dispel misperceptions about the opposite notion—that capitalism is morally inferior because it is a system of economic injustice and encourages selfishness and greed. Opposing views regarding the morality and economic justice of free enterprise usually reflect extreme polarizations of opinions, in many cases because of misunderstandings about the issues. All economic and social arrangements are morally imperfect and less than completely fair or just. Too often, however, capitalism is the "fall guy" for the wrong reasons.

The ongoing debate about economics and morality reflects the complexity as well as the emotion of differing opinions. As a result, there appears to be a lack of understanding by the general public as to how to reconcile the many apparent advantages of capitalism with the views expressed by those who attack the system on moral grounds. Attempting to dispel some of the negative ideas about captalism, even if successful, will not prove that the free market is morally superior. However, a better understanding of the issues can correct ideas held by some that capitalism is morally inferior just because it is not perfect.

Most of what follows is neither new nor original. Interpretations and emphasis of the views of others presented here reflect many personal opinions influenced by the author's friendly bias toward the free market. The main purpose is to present a concise and nontechnical summary of the key issues in the debate about the morality of the profit system.

Morality, Economic Justice, and Profits

Chapter I

The Profit System under Attack

> The idea has got around that industrial capitalism is un-
> popular and always has been, that it is the work of a tiny
> minority who have thrust it upon the reluctant mass of
> mankind. Nothing could be further from the truth.[1]

Many persons view the business community and free
enterprise as morally inferior compared to other economic systems. The profit system, according to the critics, is unjust and
reflects the exploitation of the economically disadvantaged by
wealthy business tycoons.

Antibusiness attitudes among religious groups provide re-
spectability for the negative public opinion about the profit
system. Many religious critics view the profit system as incom-
patible with their ethical ideal of society; meanwhile, they encourage increased financial support from the profits of the
business community for projects that conform to their special
view of socially desirable endeavors.

Although capitalism is not a perfect system, it provides an
economic arrangement that has increased material well-being
and reduced the level of poverty. Dreams of a more just society
are morally appealing, but are not easily translated into reality.
Blaming unemployment, poverty, and other economic ac-
tualities on capitalism and profits is an unfair accusation. His-

torical evidence clearly supports the superiority of capitalism in providing economic benefits to more people, although such benefits are not shared equally. The many benefits of capitalism are frequently overshadowed by emotional anti-business attitudes that claim the profit system inhibits moral behavior. Such criticism is meaningless unless it can be shown that replacing capitalism with another system provides equal benefits or that an alternative arrangement is so morally superior in the long run to justify reduced benefits.

The fact that business success is measured directly in money terms ("money is the root of all evil") contributes to its low moral esteem. However, it is not merely the attainment of profits, per se, that causes moral concern; it is whether economic justice is compatible with the profit motive and whether the profit motive has a negative influence on the moral character of individuals.

Specific examples of distasteful business practices are not the issue addressed here. Certainly, unethical behavior is found in the business community, as it is in all segments of society. The main concern is the notion that the market system (in a macro sense) is morally inferior, apart from specific examples of unethical business conduct.

As an example of the hostility toward capitalism, consider the following direct quotation from a publication of the Inter-Religious Task Force for Social Analysis, funded by the Episcopal Church Publishing Company, in its conclusion about capitalism:

> Bloated stomachs, refugees, chronic unemployment, crowded urban ghettos, rising taxes, the breakdown of social services to the aged, the handicapped, the imprisoned, the lack of money for schools, hospitals, mass transit, and the continuance of imperialist wars, etc., are all products of a system . . . a system which reaps excess for the few and scatters crumbs for the many.[2]

Naturally, almost everyone is sympathetic toward victims of this list of injustices. However, capitalism may not be the culprit. Do not these same injustices exist in other societies? How are they alleviated by socialism, for example? Suffering and economic disadvantage exist for some individuals and groups in all societies at all times; the conclusion that injustice and misery are more serious in a capitalist system is contrary to the record of free market experiences.

The attack against profits goes beyond specific injustices associated with profit-seeking practices. The attack against profits is also aimed at the influence of a market economy on moral behavior. The same Episcopal Church study quoted above concludes:

> We too need to explore the merits of an alternative system based not on competition and the profit motive, but on cooperation and solidarity. Socialism, by its definition, embodies these ideals and has, in a relatively short length of time, proven itself to be a viable alternative to capitalism. Granted, the specific form socialism would take in the United States, the richest country in the world, is an open question. But in light of all the severe problems we have in this country, such a discussion can not be dismissed outright as naive, unpatriotic, or even unchristian. Indeed, the burden of proof lies with those who say that capitalism here or in any country can serve the needs of the poor and powerless. The fact is that, as we have seen, it has been and continues to be the principal cause of underdevelopment and poverty in the world today.[3]

A more damning indictment of the capitalist system is hard to imagine. The accusation that capitalism is the principal cause of poverty and other social injustices is easily refuted by studying comparative economic results. Looking for ways to improve economic justice is a different issue that must be addressed by all societies regardless of actual results achieved in the past. The twofold concern about the profit system is apparent, a concern about the justice of the system and a concern about the influence of the system on moral behavior.

One of the most striking examples of the attack against the profit system comes from the Methodist Federation for Social Action in a report titled *A Critical Study of Capitalism and the Christian Faith,* which states in part:

> In keeping with the Federation's commitment to replace the present struggle-for-profit system with a just and humane one, and in keeping with the Biblical hope for a new creation, the study points toward the possibility for fundamental changes in America's social, economic, and political institutions. Our hopes point in the direction of socialism, a socialism not defined by what exists elsewhere under this name so much as by their particular possibilities in the American situation.[4]

While the Federation for Social Action surely represents a minority viewpoint, the message is clear. It would be appalling to many persons to learn that even a small amount of their tithes and offerings is channeled into direct support for the establishment of socialism. Underlying the hostility toward profits are references to an unjust system, human suffering, human needs, social services, and other morally appealing phrases.

All economic systems should seek ways to improve economic justice, and ideals, including the promises of ultimate socialism, are important in helping focus on the merits of alternatives. The essential question is one of degree, i.e., a comparison of actual capitalism with practical alternatives in terms of realized results, in the first instance, and the merit of arguments regarding the likelihood of the ultimate realization of a more just and moral society under different economic systems, in the second instance. Favoring the replacement of capitalism with some type of ideal dreamworld must be evaluated against real possibilities as well as against hopes and promises. Whether capitalism, socialism, or some other alternative offers the best prospect for the eventual realization of a more just and moral world is a key issue in the debate about economic justice and morality.

Attacking capitalism for failure to attain a perfect society is intellectually troubling, even though the system admittedly has many faults. Any legitimate attack must finally face (1) the reality of economic production and human nature in the real world of scarcity and (2) the question of whether or not the capitalist process, relative to other real or imagined economic systems, is so morally distasteful that superior performance (efficiency) is too high a price to pay for its favorable economic results.

The aforementioned *Must We Choose Sides* was sponsored by the Inter-Religious Task Force, which, in turn, receives support from various church groups. Another organization that collaborates with this group is Christians for Socialism (CFS) in the United States. In an April 1982 publication, the CFS listed their policy objectives as follows:

- We are committed to the Gospel and Socialism.
- We work for a better economic system which is committed to meeting people's needs rather than than to making profits for a few.
- We are committed to a class option—to support the interests of the poor and of working people like ourselves, not the interests of the wealthy.
- We are committed to liberate the churches from the economic and cultural bonds of capitalism and authoritarianism.
- We are opposed to racism and sexism. We support people of all social orientations.
- We are influenced in our analysis of the modern world by the

writings of Marx, Lenin, Mao Tse-tung and other progressive thinkers of our time from the ranks of the feminists, minority peoples and peoples of color, and the liberation theologians.

• We work for a socialism rooted in our U.S. democratic traditions.[5]

The Methodist Federation for Social Action in the same publication quoted earlier criticizes both the injustice of capitalism and the moral behavior it encourages:

This is, first of all, a look at *capitalism,* specifically in the United States—how it works, who benefits from its operation, and who suffers under it. Second, in keeping with the Federation's historic commitment to "reject the struggle for profit as the economic base of society" and to reject a social system based on class, racial and sexual discriminations, it is a *critical* study which measures capitalism with the plumb-line of justice in the teachings of Jesus and the Hebrew prophets.[6]

The World Council of Churches (WCC) is a worldwide organization made up of a large number of church denominations from various countries. While the council does not speak directly for its supporting members, it speaks indirectly for them and generally is a critic of capitalism on most issues. Officials of the council admit that the staff are nearly all socialists and that it is actively involved in revolutionary movements around the world that favor Marxism. According to Lefever, "In diagnosis and prescription, the WCC's liberation theology is strikingly similar to current Marxist concepts."[7]

One of the largest contributors to the World Council of Churches is the United Methodist Church. David Jessup, a Methodist layman, presented a report at the 1980 General Conference of his church in which he stated:

Most Methodist churchgoers would react with disbelief,

even anger, to be told that a significant portion of their weekly offerings were being siphoned off to groups supporting the Palestine Liberation Organization, the governments of Cuba and Vietnam, the pro-Soviet totalitarian movements of Latin America, Asia and Africa, and several violence prone fringe groups in this country.[8]

Jessup identified numerous other groups receiving Methodist funds, and according to him, "what they all have in common is a earnest desire to promote the view that America is an evil society."[9]

The acceptance of violence by the WCC and others as a legitimate means of achieving social transformation is a fairly new element in the criticism of capitalism that reinforces a 1920 attack of capitalism by the Federal Council of Churches.

Capitalism depends on the conflict between capital and labor. Capitalism treats people as tools. Capitalism relies on self-interest and the profit motive. Capitalism produces stunted personalities. Capitalism is contrary to the teaching of Christ that the human personality is sacred, that brotherhood is the proper relationship between men, that cooperation and not greed should guide men's actions, and that social behavior should be guided by loving service.[10]

Additional evidence of the attack against the profit system is readily available to the interested reader. The recent U.S. Bishops' report: *Economic Justice for All*, while not a direct attack on capitalism, presents a current discussion of the same issues and is discussed in more detail in Chapter III.

Many of the arguments against capitalism reflect an earnest hope for more economic justice and morality than found in any existing system. To that extent, criticism is helpful and constructive. In too many cases, however, the critics of capitalism rely on impressions based on the *fallacy of false*

7

cause—the tendency to place blame on the profit system merely because certain undesirable results coexist with the system. Unless those undesirable traits are found to be less severe under some attainable alternative system, critics should not condemn capitalism too harshly. In many cases, there seems to be an impression that the profit system is responsible for economic injustices that upon examination are found to be widespread in other societies. The recognition of economic injustice is one thing; attacking the profit system as the major cause of those injustices is a different issue.

The attack on the profit system by some critics is independent of the results actually experienced. They argue that capitalism encourages lower moral standards and improved efficiency may be too high a price to pay. Although this line of criticism, if factual, could be damaging to capitalism, there is no direct evidence to support this view.

Chapter II

Market and Planned Economies

All those rejecting capitalism on moral grounds as an unfair system are deluded by their failure to comprehend
what capital is, how it comes into existence and how it is
maintained, and what the benefits are, which are derived
from its employment in production processes.[1]

Only during recent times has the world experienced sus-
tainable economic growth. Until well into the Middle Ages,
most all economic activity was organized around small
productive units that were self-sufficient and largely static.
Gradually trade expanded and brought about increased
economic growth, which promoted capital accumulation.
Increased specialization and productivity, an important by-
product of capital accumulation and expanding trade,
provided the extra labor necessary to support the industrial
revolution during the latter part of the eighteenth century in
Western Europe.

    The side effects resulting from the beginning stages of in-
dustrialization are frequently cited as evidence that the emergence of market economies (capitalism) caused increased
suffering and misery. Bertrand Russell in commenting on this
situation stated that:

The industrial revolution caused unspeakable misery both in England and in America. I do not think any student of economic history can doubt that the average happiness in England in the early nineteenth century was lower than it had been a hundred years earlier; and this was due almost entirely to scientific techniques.[2]

Many critics of capitalism point to such observations as evidence of the evil effect of a market economy. A more detailed analysis of the conditions prevailing during the early stages of the industrial revolution was conducted by a group of scholars led by Prof. Frederick Hayek. As part of this analysis, Mrs. Cooke Taylor provided a description of the existing state of affairs in a letter written in 1843, in which she stated:

> Now that I have seen the factory people at their work, in their cottages and in their schools, I am totally at a loss to account for the outcry that has been made against them. They are better clothed, better fed, and better conducted than many other classes of working péople.[3]

As an overall conclusion Professor Hayek states: "While there is every evidence that great misery existed, there is none that it was greater than or even as great as it had been before."[4] There is no question that great misery existed during this period and that such misery became more readily apparent compared to the dispersed misery existing previously. However, the eventual result was that after about 1850 real wages in England gradually increased, by 1870 they were double the level of 1800, and by 1900 they had doubled again. Whether this progress resulted from market forces alone or from social legislation designed to offset the impact of market forces is debatable.

Poor working conditions during the initial stages of the industrial revolution led Karl Marx and others to conclude that laborers were exploited by the capitalist sector. Marx believed that capitalists were responsible for poor working conditions that would result in revolution and the emergence of a classless society. However, history indicates that workers in capitalist economies have enjoyed increasing real wages, improved working conditions, and a greater share of the total national income. These favorable results, however, follow at least partly from adjustments in the pure free market process caused by the conditions suggested by Marx.

Capitalism and the Concept of Wealth

Most economic historians agree that Adam Smith provided the initial framework for modern capitalism in his book titled *An Inquiry into the Nature and Causes of the Wealth of Nations,* written in 1776. Interestingly in the present context, Smith was a professor of moral philosophy, and his argument for free enterprise was a blueprint for improving the overall society.

The early development of capitalism began with the expanding market economics of medieval Europe. Modern capitalism was finally and firmly entrenched as part of the industrial revolution in the eighteenth century, primarily in Europe.

A definition of capitalism usually takes into account the production for a market by enterprising individuals for the purpose of making a profit. On the opposite extreme is a form of economic organization generally referrred to as a command economy, such as socialism, which follows largely from Marx. A widely accepted definition is one offered by Samuelson and Nordhaus:

The market mechanism is a form of economic organization in which individual consumers and businesses interact through markets to solve the central problems of economic organization. A command economy is one in which resource allocation is determined by government, commanding individuals and firms to follow the state's economic plan.[5]

As already noted, both modern capitalism and socialism fall between these extremes. It seems clear that some mix of market conditions and centralized planning is important in providing an acceptable level of economic justice. The profits and morality debate is not about the purity of one system or the other; the real argument is concerned with the tendency in one direction or the other. Choosing the correct balance must take account of actual performance and the effect of the mix on moral character.

The framework for capitalism offered by Smith challenged existing mercantilist policies of the eighteenth century in Western Europe. Mercantilism viewed wealth as a *stockpiling* of goods, mainly gold, silver, and land. The focus of the market concept advanced by Smith was on the much larger and more important issue—the creation of new wealth from increased production. While some individuals or groups will always benefit more than others, a larger total production provides an improved standard of living for society in general.

Increased wealth and a higher standard of living are not merely the result of an abundance of natural resources. One need only study the rapid economic growth of countries such as Japan, Hong Kong, South Korea, Singapore, and Taiwan, all with relatively limited natural resources, to appreciate the true nature and causes of wealth.

Increases in wealth come about from ingenuity, incentives, and increased knowledge. Increased incomes and national wealth are produced by new enterprises, such as the

Federal Express Corporation and Apple Computer. The multitude of new jobs, higher incomes, and increased spending rippling through the economy as a result of these enterprises is no less real in producing national wealth than natural resources that may lie dormant for years without producing any benefits to society.

Wealth is generally perceived to be associated with rich individuals who have managed to gain an advantage at the expense of others. The capitalist meaning of wealth refers to additional production and income that increases the well-being of society in general and not the reallocation of a stockpile of existing goods from one group to another. There is probably no greater misconception about capitalism than this confusion between national wealth and personal wealth.

As an example of the lack of understanding regarding the economic concept of national wealth, consider the following quote from a modern textbook titled *Moral Issues in Business:*

> Today's enterprising capitalists use property to create more property, to enlarge acquisition, to garner more and more wealth. As they accumulate more and more property, there is less and less for others. The relative positions of the parties with respect to property is not equal, for as one has gained the other has, of necessity, lost. And whereas what has been gained can exceed what one requires or can make good use of (except to create even more wealth for self), what is lost could well be ready access to basic necessities.[6]

It is from this vantage point that the author of the above quotation describes the nature of capitalism. The erroneous conclusion of this view is that increased national wealth accrues to a select few at the direct expense of someone else.

After analyzing the nature and causes of wealth, Smith and his followers focus on the framework most conducive for producing increased wealth for society. While capitalist and socialist systems share the objective of improving living standards, the means of achieving this goal are critically different. At the cornerstone of the capitalist system's method of increasing wealth are incentives, including profits; a command system relies on central direction by the state as the means for achieving the same goal.

In sharp contrast to central planning, a market system relies on personalized incentives as the most efficient method of creating more wealth for the total society. According to Adam Smith:

> Every individual is continually exerting himself to find out the most advantageous employment for whatever capital he can command. It is his own advantage, indeed, and not that of society, which he has in view. But the study of his own advantage naturally, or rather necessarily, leads him to prefer that employment which is most advantageous to the society.
>
> It is only for the sake of profit that man employs capital in the support of industy; and he will always, therefore, endeavor to employ it in the support of that industry of which the produce is likely to be of the greatest value.
>
> But the annual revenue of every society is always precisely equal to the exchangeable value of the annual produce of its industry. As every individual, therefore, endeavors to direct that industry where its produce will be of the greatest value, every individual necessarily labors to render the annual revenue of the society as great as he can. He generally, indeed, neither intends to promote the public interest, nor knows how much he is promoting it. By directing that industry in such a manner as its produce may be of the greatest value, he intends only his own gain, and he is in this, as in many other cases, led by an invisible hand to promote an end which was no part of his intention. Nor is it always the worse for the society that it was not part of it. By

pursuing his own interest he frequently promotes that of the society more effectively than when he really intends to promote it.[7]

Thus Smith reasons that the pursuit of one's own interest will in a roundabout way result in increased benefits for society. The invisible hand of incentives operating through a market economy serves to achieve these increased benefits, although it is indirect and unintentional. It is the incentive of self-interest that bring about the greatest overall national wealth. Although Smith was concerned with social responsibility as well as increased production, he firmly believed that personal incentives would lead to the greatest general benefit to society:

> . . . man has almost constant occasion for the help of his brethren, and it is in vain for him to expect it from their benevolence only. He will be more likely to prevail if he can interest their self-love in his favor, and show them that it is for their own advantage to do for him what he requires of them. Whoever offers to another a bargain of any kind proposes to do this; and it is in this manner that we obtain from one another the far greater part of those good offices which we stand in need of. It is not from the benevolence of the butcher, the brewer, or the baker that we expect our dinner, but from their regard to their own interest. We address ourselves, not to their humanity, but to their self-love, and never talk to them of our necessities, but of their advantages.[8]

While Smith looked upon self-interest as the best means to promote the general welfare of society, most people feel guilty about references to self-interest, especially when the guilt feelings arise from a religious perspective. Part of the reason for guilt feelings has to do with the view that selfishness and greed are encouraged by a free market, even though the increased material benefits may be favorable to the general society.

In contrast to Smith, Karl Marx argued that the value of a product (and the total production of a society, including its capital base) comes about from the labor input expended in its creation. This theory is no longer widely accepted even in socialist economies. What value does one thousand hours of labor input have for producing buggy whips? What value is labor alone in producing airplane engines, which also require the commitment of large amounts of capital at risk for long periods of time with no sure return? In a modern and specialized world where the production lead time for a product is long, who is to pay for the labor value in the interim except the capital risk taker? Who should pay the start-up expenses, including salaries and benefits, for workers of a new venture with the risk of failure? The answers to these questions are obvious and destroy any lingering fascination with a labor theory of value.

Microeconomic Aspects of a Market Economy

The role of profits in the creation of national wealth is widely misunderstood. There is a perception by many that profits arise as a result of a reduction in compensation paid to workers. This mistaken notion about profits, a holdover of the Marxian view of exploitation, ignores the nature of national wealth. More profits in the aggregate is accompanied by increased total compensation.

The dimension of risk taking is a key element in an understanding of profits. If a profit can be derived from an activity with little or no risk, then in a market economy others quickly enter that activity hoping to enjoy the risk-free profit. Additional participants tend to depress product prices and increase production costs, eventually eliminating the risk-free profit. For a temporary period of time an abnormal profit might be achieved, before others recognize the opportunity and have time to "tool-up" to supply the product or service. The abnormal profit enjoyed in the meantime, whether derived from innovation or a special market situation, reflects a willingness to take risk and incur the lost opportunity of not pursuing other activities. While the expectation of a profit is the driving force, it is not assured; many investments for profit result in disappointment.

An abnormal level of profit encourages others to increase production of the same product or service. In reviewing the outcome of this process in practice, Samuelson and Nordhaus concluded:

> The low level of corporate profitability is a puzzle to many observers. It does suggest, however, that some of the arguments about extra-ordinary monopoly power of large companies are exaggerated, and that the forces of competition among American business are powerful.[9]

The notion that profits are realized at the expense of wages is not consistent with theory or empirical evidence. The profit motive encourages additional investment and leads to increased employment and income. Thus profits and wages move together, not in an opposite direction as perceived by some critics of the profit system. A more correct perception is that "what's good for profits is usually good for workers," although the overall benefits are not equally distributed throughout the general population.

Every society must solve three basic economic problems: (1) what to produce and in what quantity; (2) how these goods and services should be produced; and (3) how the goods and services are to be distributed. These economic problems must be solved in every society, regardless of whether it favors capitalism or some other arrangement. The methods of solving these common problems differ, however. A capitalist economy emphasizes the free market mechanism of incentives, while a command-type economy attempts to direct these decisions through central planning.

The role of prices is an essential feature of capitalism in directing the invisible hand of the free market. Prices, by registering the desires of consumers, result in allocating resources to those activities in greatest demand. A product or service that can command a price sufficient to provide a profit will be offered. Profits, therefore, reflect the satisfaction of market desires. The market solution, however, may not reflect the most desirable outcome for a particular group's standard of morality or justice.

In a pure market economy, all goods and services have a price that is determined by the free interaction of the demand and supply for that product. The freely determined price serves as a vote for *what* goods and services are to be produced. If more of a product is demanded, its price rises to reflect that fact. The business sector will supply the product if it can do so and realize a profit. Competition among firms to make a profit leads to a lower cost of production (efficiency). This determines *how* the product is produced. If a particular firm realizes a profit because of innovation or greater efficiency, others will quickly make adjustments in order to also achieve a profit. Thus the role of profits is not as exploitation, but rather as the means to more efficient production of those goods and services demanded in the marketplace.

For whom things are produced is also determined by supply and demand in the markets for factors of production (labor, land, and capital). Prices are determined in the markets for each of these productive factors, and the benefits accrue to those who own them. In a market economy, the economic vote and the resulting outcome favor those with the most money votes.

A criticism of capitalism is that the free market in solving these economic problems is impersonal, resulting in an undesirable solution for some at the expense of others. In other words, the marketplace voting is not responsive to the needs of those without the effective economic means to vote. Efficiency is an important element in providing more total benefits; however, it is not the only consideration in the determination of economic justice, as we shall see later.

To repeat an earlier point, adjustments have been made in all free market economies to provide for social welfare programs under actual capitalism. Another adjustment in pure capitalism has been legislation for protection against monopoly power in order to maintain reasonably free competition in all markets. What is important is that such adjustments support but do not destroy the favorable benefits provided by the efficiency of the market economy, from which more needs are satisfied.

Every society must decide what, how, and for whom to produce. The crucial difference between a market and a planned economy is the organizing principle for making such decisions. In a market economy, prices serve as the information network for making the decisions. Without the network of freely determined prices, appointed officials or dictators must decide what is desirable based on the value judgments of some arbitrary and ultimate authority. While a market system provides what is desired, the result will not be the most desirable to everyone because of the many value judgments regarding economic benefits and burdens.

It should be remembered that every society must decide how to organize its economy. A free market is but one alternative, although it has proven to be the most efficient. The cost of selecting some other alternative is an immediate loss of economic efficiency. There may or may not be offsetting benefits, such as more economic justice or improved moral standards.

A Note on Marxism

Although our focus is capitalism, the comparison case is usually socialism. The overall framework of socialism suggested by Karl Marx is especially relevant in a discussion of economic justice.

The foundation of Marx's social and economic theories is contained in his two most famous works: *The Communist Manifesto* (1848) and *Capital* (1858). The philosophical and social history of Freidrich Hegel provided the background for Marx's concept of economic history.

Hegel described the social evolution of history as a dialectic process. According to Hegel, all history and human experience is explained by the process of a dialectical movement of opposing forces (thesis and antithesis) into a reconciling synthesis. Since history is not static, each synthesis becomes a new thesis that reacts with a new antithesis eventually leading to an improved society.

Hegel attempted to explain history and was convinced that the final realization of a better society would follow the process of social evolution. Marx believed that economics was the cornerstone of the Hegelian dialectical process; it is the struggle of opposing economic forces that creates the dialectical process in history (dialectical materialism). If economics explains the process of social evolution, then the dialectic of history presents the opportunity for effective intervention, according to Marx.

Marx rejected the notion of private property rights except for property the worker personally produced. Thus he was bitterly opposed to the owners of the means of production (bourgeoisie) who exploited the common laborers (proletariat). In Marx's view, exploitation was the consequence of capitalism.

The result of capitalist exploitation is man's alienation, which is the basic premise of Marx's social and economic theory. Capitalism separates man from his own productive activity (forced labor), and, the money-God of a capitalist system creates a passion of greed in all of society, separating man from the more important qualities of life. Marx believed that cultural life is a superstructure determined by the economic basis of society and alienation causes a poor quality of life.

The way out of the trap of alienation, according to Marx, is for workers to seize all private property and the means of production (raw communism). Man will then have regained what he has rightfully produced. Once alienation is overcome, man can then focus on the quality of life in an atmosphere of positive humanism (ultimate communism).

Marx's economic theory was essentially a framework to support his social alienation theory. At the center of his economic theory is the *labor theory of value*—the value of any product is equal to the amount of labor needed to produce it. The other part of his economics is the concept of *surplus value* (profits)—the difference between what the capitalist realizes from a product and the amount of labor value employed to produce it. Capitalism supports a higher and higher surplus value, which further alienates man from his work, according to Marx.

Whereas profit plays a positive role in a market economy, it represents exploitation in the Marxist scheme. Marx believed profits and the market system served no positive purpose and mistakenly assumed that the productive efficiency of capitalism (which he readily recognized) would not be changed once all property was in the hands of the workers themselves. As we have seen, however, it is the market system that serves the vital functions of directing the what, how, and for whom decisions of a society most effectively. Marx believed that once alienation is overcome, society would continue to function with the same efficiency, guided only by a saintly vision of "from each according to his ability, and to each according to his need."

Thus far, history has proven Marx wrong. He failed to see that both capitalist and socialist societies can change and eliminate the seriousness of the alienation that he detested; he failed to recognize the spreading influence of the middle class in society and the opportunities for enlarging the participation of laborers in the economic process itself; and finally, he offered nothing more than a vision of how society could hopefully organize itself economically. Marx failed to recognize that a state bureaucracy for making the what, how, and for whom decisions would not function as effectively as the "invisible hand" of the market process.

Despite the real world failure of actual socialism, the hope for a more just and moral society through appropriate modifications to the socialist dream is still a powerful influence in the debate over economic justice. The resentment of the profit system prevailing today reflects in no small measure the notion that desire for profits exploits workers.

It has been determined over and over in many societies that economic efficiency suffers in direct proportion to the amount of control over the economic process. As already noted, however, all societies have found it necessary to intervene to some extent in directing economic affairs. The pure market system and the socialist framework of Marx represent extreme and opposing views of the appropriate level of interference. One of the key considerations for economic justice is balancing the mix between efficiency and interference, which is discussed in later chapters.

Before going further, it is helpful to repeat one observation for clarity and emphasis: Arguments for or against the moral nature of capitalism and socialism are not, in most cases, directed only at the pure variety of either system. Each system, as actually existing today, represents many adjustments to its pure form. Thus the basic arguments in the current debate reflect varying opinions about the underlying fundamentals of one system or the other and the mix of these different elements that provide the most economic justice in the short run and long run.

Chapter III

Reasons for the Conflict

> To my great regret, I have to add the Christian Churches
> to the list of those whose social outlook now contributes
> to the subversion of Capitalism.[1]

There are many reasons for the negative attitude about the profit system. This chapter discusses some of the most significant ones.

The Religious Perspective

If there is a single theme that links the various arguments against the profit system, it probably comes from a religious perspective. The typical religious attitude toward capitalism is expressed in the following from Warren Brookes:

> It is this material utopianism which draws so many Christians to socialism, which seems to rest on the Christian ideal of the essential spiritual brotherhood, equality, goodness, and perfection of man, and which theorizes that it is only the iniquitous and discriminatory economic force of capitalism that make man behave badly. Remove these evil forces, the Christian socialist promises, and mankind's inherent goodness will

flourish in a kind of kingdom of heaven right here on earth.[2]

Many persons assume that capitalism is inconsistent with the view of justice and brotherly love described in the Bible. But is it more inconsistent with scriptural teachings than any other economic system? The message of justice found in the Scriptures is one of universal justice that relates to personal behavior regardless of the social structure of a specific society. Universal justice transcends economic structures and may be compatible with capitalism, socialism, or other systems. It is ironic that some religious critics believe capitalism is morally inferior when it appears that Christianity actually flourishes most in capitalist societies. Although the increase in well-being provided by the free market is not shared equally by everyone, material success itself need not encourage greed or destroy compassion and generosity.

Brookes in addressing the religious criticism of capitalism concludes:

> . . . the Church, in stressing human material needs so completely (needs which it has neither the resources nor the mandate to fulfill), has abdicated its unique role as spiritual feeder and focused the thought of the people, instead of on God, even more assiduously on the state (and therefore on material things and relationships) as the source of all good.[3]

The focus of the religious argument against capitalism reflects the unfavorable comparisons of actual economic systems with some utopian ideal. While a more just and moral society is always desirable, it is not capitalism that stands in the way of attaining that ideal.

William Temple, a famous Archbishop of Canterbury, stated the issue in this fashion:

It is sometimes supposed that what the Church has to do is to sketch a perfect social order and urge men to establish it. But it is very difficult to know what a "perfect social order" means. Is it the order that would work best if we were all perfect? Or is it the order that would work best in a world of men and women such as we actually are? If it is the former, it certainly ought not to be established; we would wreck it in a fortnight.[4]

Utopianism

Many critics of capitalism, including those arguing from a religious perspective, seem to favor socialism because a more just world is promised by the myth of ultimate socialism. This myth attempts to mold the parts—the entire economic, social, and political system—into a neat unitary whole. According to Peter Berger, the socialist myth is based on a comparison of utopian socialism (spiritual) with actual socialism (economic system).[5]

One may view Marxism as a secularized version of the biblical view of history as consisting of a fall from grace, a set of redemptive events embodied in a human community, and leading up to a great climax that will bring ordinary history to an end. Marxism substituted private property for original sin, the revolutionary process for God's redemptive activity, the proletariat for the Church, and the attainment of communism for the advent of the Kingdom of God. Berger concludes that "one reason for the perduring appeal of Marxism is that it seems to allow its adherents to eat their cake and have it too. It is an appeal that is hard to beat."[6]

In a world of scarcity, choices must be made and trade-offs accepted. While one can accept utopian socialism as a desirable goal, actual socialism must face economic reality, like all other systems. It is impossible to escape the inevitable conclusions that resources are always limited (in terms of providing everything desired by all) and that wants are insatible and constantly changing in every society.

The link between practical socialism and utopian socialism is mainly by name associaton only. The utopian promise has not emerged from raw communism anywhere in the world. Indeed, real world socialism has generally produced abusive power struggles that undermine human rights while performing poorly in providing economic benefits.

Liberation Theology

An extreme view of the religious attitude toward profits is liberation theology. This viewpoint is not based on the idealistic appeal of utopian socialism; it is an argument for actual socialism. The underlying theme is that poverty and social injustices are *caused* by capitalism and that Christians should become politically active in replacing capitalism. Blaming capitalism for poverty and injustice is an extreme example of the *fallacy of false cause*. The poor and oppressed are not unique to capitalist societies. There is no evidence that socialism is superior in actually improving living standards or reducing poverty; all available evidence points to the opposite conclusion.

The fundamental argument of liberation theology is that Christians are commanded by the Scriptures to become politically active on behalf of the poor and oppressed. While this viewpoint is closely related to the typical religious criticism of capitalism, it is more extreme and pushes the argument to the area of political activism. That Christians (and all persons with a sense of universal justice) should become actively involved in aiding the poor and oppressed is not the issue; the real issue

27

is, How are the poor helped most in reality?

Some liberation theologians suggest that God is on the side of the poor and oppressed. Whether one accepts this view or not, it is difficult to understand why socialism should be the preferred vehicle based on a comparison of actual results. Moreover, there is no evidence that socialist societies create a greater desire on the part of individuals for assisting the disadvantaged.

Semantics and Misperceptions

Another reason for the apparent conflict between morality and the profit system is the economic language used to describe the nature of capitalism. This is best illustrated by reference to a few of the key words used to characterize capitalism—*wealth, selfishness, greed, profits,* and *competition*—words that project negative impressions.

Wealth is commonly thought of as personal monetary richness, selfishness and greed are typically associated with a lack of compassion and caring for others, and profits and competition are perceived as exploitation of the masses by wealthy tycoons. These semantic misperceptions give critics of capitalism an illusionary advantage when arguing against the moral character of the profit system. The nature of wealth in the context of capitalism has already been discussed. True wealth in a capitalist sense is not about personal richness or fortunes; it is about the economic well-being of society on the whole.

Selfishness and *greed* are probably the most negative expressions associated with capitalism. In everyday usage, *selfishness* and *greed* imply an unrelenting pursuit to gain personal advantage over others. The capitalist meaning of these terms has to do with providing incentives that operate through the "invisible hand" of the marketplace to serve the common good of the total society. The argument that a market economy encourages more greed and selfishness, and whether or not such behavior represents lower moral standards, is much more than a semantic misperception. Further elaboration of this issue will be dealt with after a discussion of the philosophical aspects of capitalism and economic justice.

Business Ethics

Specific examples of business activities contribute to a credibility problem for capitalism. From the robber baron days of the late nineteenth and early twentieth centuries to the current Wall Street insider-trading cases, the business community frequently faces moral criticism. It is not difficult to find examples of business practices to support the arguments of those prone to label the profit system and capitalism as morally inferior. What goes unnoticed many times is that most of the millions of business decisions made everyday cannot be labeled as unethical. It is a mistake to condemn the entire market system for the unethical practices of a few.

Business ethics is part of ethics in general—like religious ethics or medical ethics. It only has meaning as ethics applied to business, not as a special code of behavior. If certain practices in business are unethical, then those committing such acts should be judged on the same ethical scale as others, not on some "special purpose" scale. Individual businessmen fall along the same ethical value scale as the clergy, physicians, professors, lawyers, and unskilled workers. Peter Drucker, a professor of social science and management who previously taught philosophy and religion, states:

There is only one ethics, one set of rules of morality, one

code, that of individual behavior in which the same rules apply to everyone alike. Viewed from the mainstream of traditional ethics, business ethics is not ethics at all, whatever else it may be. For it asserts that acts that are not immoral or illegal if done by ordinary folk become immoral or illegal if done by business.[7]

Examples of questionable ethical conduct can be found in every segment of society. However, we are concerned here with the morality of the overall market system, not with isolated examples of unethical behavior found in the business community.

Extravagance

Extravagance is sometimes viewed as an expression of selfishness and greed. The usual meaning of *extravagant* is "lavish, wasteful, or imprudent in the spending of money." When attempting to define *lavish* or *wasteful,* one immediately confronts the question of, Compared to what? If I criticize someone who appears extravagant by my standards, I must, in turn, accept criticism from others who believe my habits to be extravagant by their standards. Some of the most vocal critics of American capitalism would themselves be considered extravagant by a large percentage of the world's population.

Those who criticize wealth fail to realize the direct benefits provided by the rich. Michael Novak argues that many of the aesthetic amenities longed for under socialism are in practice provided in capitalism by the wealthy. The rich provide benefits, according to Novak, because:

Their mushy ideological sentiments lead them, often enough, to endow foundations which sponsor scholars who write in favor of overturning the system. Not a few museums, galleries, symphony halls and libraries owe their non-bureaucratic liberties and real human contributions to the grand ambitions of the rich for public immortality. . . . Not a few of the basic industries of modernity owe their origins to the curiosity and perseverance of a rich man in his fascination with a problem or a gadget. Most new technologies are supported in their infancy by marketing strategies aimed first at the rich and then at the masses.[8]

Every society has a group of lavish and extravagant inhabitants. Extravagance is not unique to capitalism.

Poverty

Another issue in the profits and morality debate deals with poverty. While, on average, America now enjoys the highest standard of living in history, there are many individuals and families who are poor. Often forgotten, but the flip side of the same issue is; how many more Americans would be below the poverty level today if the average standard of living had not grown steadily over a long period of time as a result of the free market?

While trying to be careful not to line up too strongly on either side of the argument, the 1986 U.S. Bishops' Pastoral Message and Letter titled *Economic Justice for All: Catholic Social Teaching and the U.S. Economy*[9] is an indirect expression of the core conflict described above.

The Bishops praise the performance of the U.S. economy in numerous passages, and are careful not to present a direct indictment of capitalism. Most persons can find much to agree with in the Bishops' presentation, whether from a Christian viewpoint as traced through the Bible, or from a humanitarian feeling of caring for others, aside from any particular religious persuasion. Helping those in need transcends rigid religious boundaries and appeals to the moral goodness inherent in most people.

After outlining a Christian vision of economic life, the Bishops list a number of economic ills. Their focal point, throughout, is from the vantage point of the poor and disadvantaged. A host of economic maladies contribute to the Bishops' concern—unemployment, the family farm, inequality, minimum wages, economic growth, inflation, international trade and balance of payments, and other issues.

Again, one finds difficulty in disagreeing with the separate desirability of each of these economic goals. In fact, the Bishops would have been well served to include in their message a review of the U.S. Employment Act of 1946 and the Humphrey-Hawkins Act of 1978, each representing legislation of the U.S. Congress to achieve the goals of full employment, price stability, and growth. Agreement on independent goals is easier than deciding on how all competing desires can be achieved.

Economics is concerned with the allocation of scarce resources among competing uses. This is true in any type economic system. How is it the Bishops purpose to provide employment for everyone willing to work, and at the same time increase minimum wages? And, at the same time, avoid inflation? Do the Bishops believe that preservation of the family farm as a way of life is more or less important than reducing world hunger from increased productive efficiency of larger farms? Do the Bishops think that lower costs of foreign production resulting in lower consumer prices in this country is more or less desirable than the closing of a plant in some local community?

In fairness, the Bishops forthrightly state that they have no specific blueprint. One must wonder, therefore, about the message. The significant message must be contained in statements such as this:

> The economy should serve people, and not the other way around. As followers of Christ we are challenged to make a fundamental option for the poor—to speak for the voiceless, to defend the defenseless, to assess lifestyles, policies and social institutions in terms of their impact on the poor. This option for the poor does not mean pitting one group against another, but rather, strengthening the whole community by assisting those who are most vulnerable. As Christians, we are called to respond to the needs of all our brothers and sisters, but those with the greatest needs require the greatest response.[10]

In summary, the closest thing to an overall policy statement in the bishops' report is contained in the following quote:

> The precarious economic situation of so many people and so many families calls for examination of U.S. economic arrangements. Christian conviction and the American promise of liberty and justice for all give the poor and the vulnerable a special claim on the Nation's resources. They also challenge all members of the Church to help build a more *just society*.[11]

The best means of building a more just society has been debated for centuries. How this goal can be accomplished is the key question. Thus far in history, actual capitalism has proved to be the best long-term option for the poor. The Bishops do not tell us how the most vulnerable are to be assisted, who is to decide on the definition of needs, and how those needs should be administered. Although the market economy itself does not target aid for the poor as its primary objective, actual capitalism makes the strongest case for the poor in terms of results. It is difficult to see how the lack of direct targeting of the poor is morally inferior when the results of free enterprise are superior in actually providing increased benefits to the most people, including the poor.

Most people desire to help those in need, and the Bishops' report focuses on the plight of the disadvantaged. Although capitalism seems to offer the best practical option for the poor, the desire for greater economic justice requires continued debate if further improvements are to be accomplished. While the Bishops' report serves this end, suggesting that capitalism is the cause of poverty is an unfair conclusion. Would there be more or less poverty if capitalism was replaced?

Inequality

It is not merely the existence of poverty that is at issue; the conflict also revolves around the uneven share of economic benefits among individuals and between various segments of society. Strangely enough, this issue in the conflict would not exist if everyone enjoyed close to the same benefits, even if the result was that everyone lived in poverty. Capitalism did not bring inequality about; inequality has always existed. Those who take an anticapitalism stand must favor some amount of inequality, since the self-interest desire of personal gain creates incentives that raise the average standard of living. The question then becomes, where is the dividing line and who decides?

The ideal of economic equality is more appealing from a purely religious standpoint than an emphasis on increased well-being for society in general. While the emotion of the equality argument is more personal and at first appealing, such attempts may result in less for everyone. True national wealth relates to the incentives and desires that result in increased incomes in the aggregate. The emotionally appealing argument of the market critics is shortsighted if the attempt to equalize hampers the incentive to create additional production. In other words, there is a trade-off between equality and efficiency, and it is the misconception about this trade-off that sometimes gives rise to the notion that a market system is unjust. In discussing this trade-off, Samuelson and Nordhaus state:

> . . . experience has shown that in some cases the distortions due to interference can become so great that the attempt to help one social class at the expense of another can end in hurting them both. Or, in the opposite case, an action that looks like it is aimed to benefit the rich finally ends by benefiting all.[12]

The question of inequality is one of the key issues in the debate over economic justice and will be discussed separately in Chapter V. Is it just for some to have more than others? Is it just for some to live in poverty while others enjoy luxury and extravagance?

Profits and Wages

There is a widely held view that profits come about at the expense of wages and directly cause poverty, inequality, and extravagance. This is largely an empirical question, which is examined in the next chapter. We will discover from the historical evidence that profits and compensation are complementary. Profit is derived from economic activity that creates income and material well-being in the process. And although profit is one of the motivating factors that drives the capitalist system, profit turns out to be a relatively small portion of the total process. The by-product of profits is an improved standard of living in the aggregate. Since the free market solution is indirect and imperfect, it is tempting to suggest that a more direct alternative for accomplishing economic justice is better. The by-product of many experiments at direct approaches to distributive justice has always been a lower average standard of living.

Historical Results and Philosophical Arguments

Most of the reasons for the resentment of capitalism can be debated from both an empirical and a philosophical point of view. While historical results generally favor capitalism, there are many misperceptions regarding the empirical evidence. The next chapter summarizes some of the facts about the results of capitalism. Chapter V offers a view of some of the philosophical issues concerning the morality and economic justice of capitalism.

Chapter IV

The Historical Results of Capitalism

> Capitalism provides the optimal context for the productive power of modern technology. To date, there are no empirically available counter-cases.[1]

Capitalism is a recent phenomenon that has been unique in providing increased standards of living. Prior to the development of industrial capitalism, economic growth was limited, with subsequent declines almost always eliminating any gain that was achieved. Only since the emergence of capitalism has the world economy experienced sustained economic growth. Paul Johnson states:

> In short, after nearly five recorded millennia of floundering about in poverty, humanity suddenly in the 1780s began to hit on the right formula, industrial capitalism. Judged simply by its capacity to create wealth and to distribute it, capitalism is a phenomenon unique in world history.[2]

By almost any measure, the increased living standards resulting from American free enterprise has been enormous. Peter Berger observes:

Whether one looks at sheer life expectancy (surely the most basic aspect of any standard of living), the incidence of diseases, nutrition, the prices of basic commodities and the resultant accessibility of inexpensive consumer goods, housing, clothing, leisure, transportation or communications—even the American poor today enjoy a standard of living which, for most of human history, would have been beyond the dreams of all but royalty.[3]

Different gauges are utilized for recording economic growth. The broadest measure is Gross National Product (GNP), a reflection of total economic activity. Table I, at the end of this chapter, shows GNP for the United States in 1986 for each of the major segments of the economy.

A second way of measuring the overall magnitude of the economy, and for viewing profits in perspective, is National Income (NI), which reflects payments to various segments involved in the production of GNP. As indicated in Table I, the two measures are essentially equivalent, except for two minor adjustments: GNP includes depreciation (which does not reflect a current outlay) and indirect business taxes (which are taxes such as the sales tax, collected by businesses on behalf of the government). Profit is the balancing item that causes GNP and NI to be equivalent, after accounting for depreciation and indirect taxes. In 1986, corporate profits before taxes were less than 7 percent of total GNP.

GNP and NI reflect the total size of the economy for a particular time period measured. Two adjustments must be made in GNP and NI to get a true picture of the trend in the average standard of living. In the first place, the effect of higher prices (inflation) must be considered, since the numbers representing GNP and NI for each year include the impact of changing prices. Adjusting for price changes provides a measure of real GNP and real NI, or the quantity of production and income apart from changes in prices. Second, it is necessary to consider growth in population in order to measure the amount of output available, on average, for each person. Real GNP and NI per capita are good indicators of the trend in the standard of living over time. Of course, average per capita GNP or NI does not reveal anything about how the average is distributed within the population.

Table II provides an indication of the size of various economies and shows real per capita GNP for selected years since 1975, expressed in 1983 (inflation-adjusted) dollars. Only GNP is shown, since NI bears a consistent relationship to GNP and reveals the same trend. The United States has the highest per capita GNP among the selected countries with comparable data. Sweden, with a heavy emphasis on social welfare policies, is ranked second.

Although historical data are not displayed in Table II, this steady economic progress in the United States extends over a long period of time. What cannot be concluded from the per capita GNP numbers is the quality or desirability of the increased standard of living and its distribution. Of course, every person has a different opinion about the quality of life and the appropriate distribution of benefits. The aggregate numbers merely reflect the increased means to satisfy higher levels of expenditures in total and not how such spending is allocated among different products and between individuals.

Samuel McCracken, the assistant to the President of Boston University, has examined in detail the changes in American living standards since the beginning of the nineteenth century. He states:

> The fact remains that the working-class American enjoys access to the good things of life in a measure unparalleled in human history, anywhere or anytime, and this fact in itself has egalitarian implications. Put simply, industrial capitalism in

America (and in other advanced societies of the capitalist type) has vastly raised the standard of living of virtually everyone in the society. For many, this fact in itself is tantamount to saying that American society is one of high equality and that it is the incredibly productive economy of American capitalism to which this achievement must be credited.[4]

Real per capita GNP is a convenient way of comparing the standard of living between countries, as also shown in Table II. A comparison of life expectancy, infant mortality, population per physician, and higher education enrollments provides additional information about the standard of living (Table III). When the pure dollar and cents profile of real per capita GNP is considered along with these other indicators, the superior well-being of the United States and other free market economies becomes readily apparent.

A Comparison with Other Countries

Some critics claim the American experience to be unique because of an abundance of natural resources. As discussed earlier, however, a nation's wealth is not dependent on natural resources, but more on incentives and aspirations. The rapid growth of Japan since World War II and the more recent success stories in East Asia (Hong Kong, South Korea, Taiwan, and Singapore) all with relatively scarce natural resources, add additional credence to the argument for capitalism. Berger, in analyzing capitalism in these East Asian economies, states that:

East Asia confirms the superior capacity of industrial capitalism in raising the material standard of living of large masses of people.

East Asia confirms the positive relation between industrial capitalism and the emergence of a class system characterized by relatively open social mobility.[5]

Even more so than in the United States, these Asian success stories illustrate that the nature and causes of national wealth are not dependent on a nation's natural resource base.

As a contrast case study, Berger compares industrial socialism in the USSR to industrial capitalism. Apart from propagandists of the Soviet regime, most observers of the Soviet economy have been struck by its inefficiency and low productivity, despite the enormous resources of the country and the coercive methods at the disposal of the regime. The centralized planning process characteristic of socialism creates a vast bureaucracy that institutionalizes inefficiency. "Most economists," Berger states, "argue that this problem (bureaucracy) is built-in precisely because the information provided by the price system has been removed."[6] A capitalist system is much more efficient because of the mechanism of market-determined prices and profits in allocating resources. This is in sharp contrast to allocations based on the bureaucracy required by a centrally planned economy.

Some critics argue that a planned economy is sometimes superior because inflation and unemployment are reduced or eliminated. Inflation, at least in the open, may appear to be less severe in a planned economy because prices are controlled. This doesn't mean, however, that everyone can purchase anything desired at a set price; it might mean that only a rationed amount, or nothing at all, can be purchased at the controlled price. This leads to rationing or an under-the-table black market.

Likewise, in a planned economy unemployment may not be as apparent, since full employment of all labor is required as part of the centrally directed plan. Full employment, however, may not lead to efficient employment; full employment may be achieved, but with enormous underemployment. The ultimate test depends on the importance of maximizing production compared with maximizing employment, even with less production. Both are important, as indicated by the twin goals in most countries of overall growth and low unemployment.

Inflation and unemployment are not completely unrelated, since at or close to full employment less efficient workers produce a declining marginal output. With capitalism, the result may be higher market prices; in a planned economy, reported inflation may be less obvious, since prices are strictly controlled. But in a controlled situation, many products may not be available at the set price.

In recent years, the Soviet economy has grown very little. Samuelson states the reasons to be: little penchant for major innovation, a string of disastrous harvests, increasing burdens of military spending, much higher costs of producing energy in the Far East and northern portions of the USSR, and the strain of using a cumbersome planning apparatus to deal with the demands of a more complicated economy.[7] More and more countries operating under central planning are turning to free market incentives in order to increase the standard of living.

The *Economist,* in an article titled "The Soviet Economy," dated April 9, 1988, summarizes the situation. According to this article, the Soviet economy has experienced no growth during the past twenty years, despite the earlier promises of Khrushchev to overtake the United States. With zero growth, the increasing Soviet population lags behind the United States in almost all areas of consumer spending. Table IV presents some startling examples for the United States, the USSR, and selected other countries. The United States in 1985 had only 1.8 persons per automobile, while the USSR had 24 persons per automobile; the United States had 76 telephones per 100 people, compared to only 11 in the USSR; the United States had 798 televisions per 1,000 people, compared to 296 for the USSR.

The Soviet economy has not performed under the heavy-handed bureaucracy of centralized planning. *Perestroika,* the economic restructing plan, is attempting to improve results through increased incentives and localized decision making. While the Soviets have not adopted capitalism, they have identified the importance of incentives in raising living standards. Realizing the benefits of personal incentives in the absence of private property rights and a free flow of capital is doubtful, however.

A March 29, 1988, article in the *Commercial Appeal* (Memphis, Tennessee), taken from the New York Times News Service, reported a similar reorganization of the Chinese government:

> China announced that its central government would be drastically reorganized to encourage efficiency and better decision making. Song Ping, a member of the Communist Party Politburo, said the defects of the current government set up have become conspicuous. Among their shortcomings, he said, are an irrational bureaucracy, too great attention to details, insufficient control, overlapping institutions, over-staffing and low efficiency. The enterprises themselves will assume responsibility for their own management and profitability.[8]

Examples of the poor performance of planned economies are numerous. Gary Becker, writing in the June 23, 1987, issue of *Business Week,* reported on a study by Professors Robert Summers and Alan Heston of the University of Pennsylvania. They analyzed seventy African countries that chose the socialist system following World War II. Those countries grew much less in terms of per capita income than did other countries over the same period.

An abundance of evidence cutting across the space of time and national boundaries clearly suggests a market-based economy is the superior performer. In general, one can say that an economy propelled by personal incentives rather than a bureaucratic and patterned ordering of the economic process is the essential difference in achieving greater efficiency.

The historical evidence is clear: industrial capitalism has achieved rapid advances in economic well-being compared to other economic systems, including modern industrial socialism. There is very little argument about the superior economic results of the free market.

A Look at Poverty

The existence of poverty is one of the important issues in the debate over the justice of a market economy. The percent of the U.S. population below the official poverty level, as determined by the Federal Government, has dropped from above 22 percent in 1959 to below 14 percent in 1986 (see Table V). While this progress may be partially related to governmental assistance programs, the decline in the poverty rate is due largely to economic growth.

The growth in real GNP and the level of the unemployment rate (Table V) reflect an expanding economy throughout the 1960's, and the poverty level was cut in half. By contrast, in the mid-1970's and again in the early 1980's, the poverty rate increased as the economy slowed down or declined. Since 1983, the economy has expanded and the poverty rate has again declined. It would appear that direct governmental redistribution policies to reduce poverty are hard to achieve in a no-growth or declining economy regardless of the desire to help the poor.

Median family income for the entire population is shown

44

in Table VI. The median level in 1985 was $27,144. As shown, however, there is a wide gap in median income between whites and nonwhites.

Family income used to determine whether or not a family is below the poverty level includes only money incomes; noncash aid such as food stamps, housing, and medical care is omitted. If these noncash payments are considered, the U.S. Census Bureau estimates that the poverty rate in 1986 would have been 9.0 percent rather than the reported 13.6 percent (see Table V).

Table VII provides a profile of persons considered poor. The overall poverty rate is influenced greatly by the very young, race, and families being headed by a female with no husband present. Looking at poverty from the standpoint of the family, Table VIII reveals that those with a young householder and little education have an especially high incidence of poverty. As Table IX shows, poverty also varies by region of the country.

As indicated earlier, the official definition of poverty is expressed as a money income level excluding the value of noncash benefits. In addition, it must be noted that those below the poverty level earn some amount of income. Taking account of these factors, the total poverty gap is somewhere between $32 billion and $43 billion, about 1 percent of GNP (Table X). By contrast, total social welfare expenditures in the United States in 1985 were $729 billion, about 18.5 percent of GNP. Of this amount, $140 billion represented either cash or noncash benefits received by persons above and below the poverty line who made no payment and rendered no service in return for the benefits received (Tables XI and XII).

Many doubts and arguments can be raised about the size of the poverty gap. However, it can be said that the profit-based system of the U.S. economy has been generous, with 18.5 percent of GNP representing social welfare expenditures and 3.5 percent of GNP allocated to free benefits based only on a demonstrated need of assistance.

In terms of progress against poverty, Nicholas Eberstadt, a visiting Fellow at Harvard University, has examined poverty in communist and noncommunist countries. He concludes:

> . . . there is little reason to think the performance of Marxist-Leninist governments in attending to the poor has been generally superior to that of the non-communist governments against which they might reasonably be compared. In facilitating the reduction of poverty and the spread of prosperity, markets appear to offer two single advantages: they possess an inherent ability to transmit information, and they stimulate mobility.[9]

Income Inequality

Poverty is a special case in the more general argument over the justice of an uneven distribution of income. Median family income in the U.S. in 1985 was $27,144, which means that one-half of the families had incomes above this level and one-half below this level. This is a first rough measure of the inequality of incomes. However, the incomes in each half are not evenly distributed; some families fall on the extremes and some in between. One way of further dissecting the number is to look at a breakdown by quintile rankings. Table XIII shows such a breakdown.

The 20 percent of U.S. families with the lowest income receive about 5 percent of total family income, while the highest 20 percent receive about 40 percent. If income were evenly distributed, each quintile would receive 20 percent. Tracing the lowest 20 percent number back to the early 1940's in the United States shows that this quintile has remained about constant in terms of the percentage of income received.[10] Thus the distribution of income has not changed significantly. Referring to a previous comment, however, significant progress has been made in reducing the rate of poverty. Most observers would acknowledge that absolute equality is not a realistic goal; where then between these two extremes is the most appropriate level? There is no concrete answer to this question, only subjective judgments based largely on comparisons.

Table XIII shows the distribution of income by quintile groups and for the highest 10 percent for several countries. As indicated by examination of this table, income distribution in the United States is not much different from that in other countries. The often heard comment that income distribution in the United States is more unequal than in controlled economies is not supported by the evidence.

Inequality of incomes is very apparent in planned economies. Many who postulate the inferior moral nature of capitalism do so based on the notion that it is the greed of capitalism that produces a wide degree of income inequality. Facts do not support this notion. Samuelson and Nordhaus state that "the ratio of the average income of the top 10 percent of the population to the bottom 10 percent is only slightly greater in the United States than in the U.S.S.R., and in Great Britain the same ratio is only one-half of the U.S.S.R." They conclude "that when incomes of the communist elite are included, the degree of inequality in the USSR is strikingly similar to that of the U.S."[11] Peter Berger states:

> In sum, whatever else may be said about stratification in real existing socialism it has not brought anything like the egalitarian income distribution desired by most socialists. Probably income distribution does not differ much from that in the society of western industrial capitalism; it may be somewhat more unequal.[12]

According to recent reports, the magnitude of poverty in the USSR is much greater than previously acknowledged:

> . . . the Soviet authorities who once denied that poverty existed in their country and pronounced it an evil of capitalism now say at least 20 percent of the population live in poverty. There is no state plan for dealing with poverty, according to interviews with Soviet officials. There is no government agency to which people in need can turn.[13]

Factual information dispels the notion of those who claim actual capitalism is morally inferior, or that actual socialism is morally superior, based on poverty levels and the inequality of incomes. The fact is that industrial capitalism has achieved a higher rate of economic growth and improved living standards over time than has industrial socialism and with no greater inequality of income. The average standard of living under capitalism has increased, and all income groups have participated to varying degrees, i.e., all groups have experienced increasing average incomes.

For whatever reasons, inequality is a reality. If less inequality is a worthy social objective, policies can be implemented to achieve more equality. But the cost will be a lower overall income level. In a capitalist system, the appropriate policy for reducing inequality might be a more progressive taxation system. In a centrally planned economy, the policy might be direct allocation of income. We have already seen that income distribution in the USSR is not much different than in the United States, the average income level is much lower in the USSR, and more poverty exists in the USSR. To the extent that a policy designed to reduce inequality results in less efficiency, a lower output, and slower growth, the policy will be counterproductive, i.e., the total income pie will decrease or not grow as rapidly. As indicated previously, this may very well result in a higher incidence of poverty, since economic growth tends to reduce the level of poverty. Rebecca Blank, in a study of the effect of growth on income distribution, reached the following conclusion: "This study confirms that the income distribution narrows (tends to more equality) in times of economic growth."[14]

Redistribution policies, whether through taxation or direct allocation, affect personal incentives and lead to less efficiency. And despite the ideal of utopian socialism expressed by Karl Marx, "to each according to need, and from each according to ability," a reduction in personal incentives results in less economic growth. The new direction of economic policy in the Soviet Union is designed around stimulating incentives as a means of encouraging growth.

Not only has the market system in the United States raised the average standard of living, it has also provided the opportunity for worker mobility within the economy. In other words, in the American economy one is not relegated to the status quo based on the selection of parents. Connor has found that the market system indeed offers an opportunity for mobility, but the mobility works in both directions:

> Close to one-third of sons from the upper manual stratum and close to one-fourth from the lower manual stratum reach elite status (that is move into the upper white-collar stratum). Even more interestingly, the majority of persons in the elite originated below the manual/non-manual divide, and that majority is increasing over time (51.6% in 1962, 54.1% in 1973) . . . it is *less* of an advantage to start out at the top, less of a handicap to start out at the bottom.[15]

A University of Michigan study of poverty over a ten-year period found that only 17 percent of the poor had been in poverty for as long as two years running.[16] Economic growth coupled with mobility and freedom provides the best option for those below the poverty level to rise again. In a growing economy where the average level of income is increasing, some persons experience a smaller increase in income, some an absolute decline, and others a more abundant increase than the average. A higher growth rate in the average, however, provides the opportunity for those below the poverty level to emerge from the poverty trap, as suggested by the Connor and University of Michigan studies.

Again, some critics of capitalism claim that the American experience is unique and is not representative of what might be expected in other countries. Berger, in examining data for the East Asia case, found a pattern similar to the United States, as previously noted. A similar analysis was performed by Papanck. Papanck distinguishes between three existing development models: (1) capitalist or market-oriented; (2) market-oriented but with government intervention to bring about redistributionist effects; and (3) "populist," with substantial government ownership.

The conclusions reached by Papanek are very revealing. He found that:

> The higher the rate of growth the more rapid the passage from very low incomes, where income distribution is egalitarian, through middle incomes, where it tends to be un-equally distributed, to the level of a developed country, which again tends to be egalitarian. This tendency for per capita income and income distribution to be related seems to explain only a small part of the large difference in equality among nations. If one examines particular countries over time there is even less evidence that it exists at all. A comparison of countries, therefore, does not provide much support for the argument that government needs to intervene in the economy to prevent a worsening of income distribution in the early stage of development.[17]

Whereas some observers have argued that a policy of government intervention at the middle income level is appropriate in order to prevent a move toward more inequality, Papanck finds that this might only inhibit the progress toward the third and more egalitarian stage.

Papanck goes on to state that:

> The purer the capitalism, the more rapid the growth on the whole and the more labor intensive the commercial sector. The outcome was less favorable for growth, income distribution, and poverty when capitalism was modified. The result was inefficient, high cost, capital intensive development that created little employment. Populist regimes distorted labor and capital prices even more, because widespread nationalization increased the role of decision makers for whom the price of capital was close to zero, while labor was more costly.[18]

The policy prescription recommended by Papanck is relying on market incentives, but with government intervention to compensate for market imperfections. In other words, Papanck might modify the role of the free market to temporarily reduce tensions in a poor society, but he would be careful to preserve the incentives of the free market because of its longer-term benefits of economic growth and improved equality.

Another issue in the inequality discussion is the relative standard of living. While we have found that the best option for the poor in terms of the standard of living is capitalism, the progress toward this objective creates a recognition of expectations on the part of those who see others doing better. In other words, expectations result in dissatisfactions. The implication is that an inequality gap might be more acceptable if there is no hope of altering one's status quo postition, while the same gap at a higher overall standard of living level is unacceptable once there is an expectation of improvement.

51

It is important to understand that it is the expectation of an improved relative standard of living that provides the incentives for a market-driven economy. And we have seen from the American experience of mobility and the cross-country analysis by Papanck that this is an important condition for ultimately realizing the goal of a higher standard of living for more people.

Much of the criticism from the modern Church, including the Bishops' report on economic justice, appears in the final analysis to be mainly concerned with the concept of relative well-being. Then, from a standpoint of worldwide social justice, we should turn most of our social concern toward the truly dismal poverty of the very poorest countries (see Tables II and III) and be less concerned over the relatively higher living standards of even the poorest in the United States.

However, the best option for the poor is economic growth, which in the long run results in improved benefits to more persons. Hayek, speaking of expectations in *The Constitution of Liberty*, states:

> Yet a progressive society, while it relies on this process of learning and imitation, recognizes the desires it creates only as a spur to further effort. It does not guarantee the results to everyone. It disregards the pain of unfilled desire aroused by the example of others. It appears cruel because it increases the desire of all in proportion as it increases its gifts to some. Yet so long as it remains a progressive society, some must lead and the rest must follow.[19]

Another issue in the concern over inequality is the relationship between profits and wages. A review of Table I shows where profits rank in the overall economic scheme: it is only one of the factors of production. In 1986, profits represented 8.3 percent of NI, while compensation of employees accounted for 73.2 percent of NI.

If the notion that profits are realized at the expense of wages was valid, then during periods of more rapid economic growth and increasing profits we would expect to find profits growing more rapidly and becoming larger relative to NI. Just the opposite has occurred. Table XIV provides information on the growth in profits and compensation from 1950 to 1985. On the average, for the entire thirty-five-year period, profits increased 5.9 percent per year and compensation grew 8.1 percent per year. Table XV shows profits and compensation as percentages of NI back to 1950. The profits percentage has generally declined, while compensation has increased. The clear indication from evidence shown in Tables XIV and XV is that economic growth has benefited workers on the average.

An analysis of the up and down movements in business activity since 1950 reveals that profits as a percentage of NI (which steadily declined over this time period) experienced a setback during each business contraction. On the other hand, compensation as a percentage of NI dropped only modestly during the 1953–54 and 1957–58 recessions and increased during the other five recessions occurring since 1950.

Business investments, with their risks, obviously require a higher return than a no-risk investment. Of course, it is not the return in any one year that is critical, but the return over a period of years. The perception of enormously high profits by large corporations must be viewed relative to the stockholders' investment at risk and not merely the absolute amount of profits. *Forbes Magazine* reports that during the five-year period 1982–86, a period of economic expansion, the return on equity for the largest U.S. companies averaged 12.6 percent. By comparision, the average yield on no-risk U.S. Government bonds during the same period was 10.7 percent for five-year bonds, 10.97 percent for ten-year bonds, and 11.11 percent for twenty-year bonds.[20] A positive spread in favor for business investments is required to compensate for the added risk. The positive spread indicated above does not appear extraordinarily large.

Poverty in the United States is not just a function of benevolence; it is also a question of the priority of expenditures. This is best illustrated by reference to Table XVI. About 25 percent of America's GNP is accounted for by Federal Government expenditures. As stated earlier, it would take only about 1 percent of GNP to bring everyone above the poverty level. The political allocation of Federal Government spending (also shown for major categories in Table XVI) falls outside the realm of free enterprise.

Charity

It is also instructive to look at total giving in the United States by corporations, foundations, and individuals. Table XVII shows the amounts of private philanthropy in 1986 and how it was allocated. While total giving is directed to many different uses, reported donations exceed the estimated size of the poverty gap.

The *Economist* recently reported that "Americans give a far bigger proportion of their incomes to charity, and volunteer more of their time, than do people anywhere."[21]

It is largely the higher incomes produced by the American profit-based system that allow 2 percent of GNP to flow into private philanthropy. However, it is not the free market system that determines how these funds are allocated. Religion alone received $40.9 billion from private giving in 1986, an amount equal to the poverty gap. Free enterprise, which provides the source of the philanthropy, is not the culprit in the poverty problem.

This is not the place to discuss the appropriate allocation

of funds available from charity. Religious organizations decide to devote part of their financial resources to outreach programs and bricks and mortar in order to spread the message of the gospel in hopes of improved future benefits. Whether one agrees or disagrees with the allocation, the Church is "investing in the future" for what is assumed to be a favorable return on investment. This is similar to corporations reinvesting a portion of current profits to achieve increased production in the future for the benefit of all.

Poverty is, of course, a real, existing problem in every economy. In the aggregate, the magnitude of poverty in capitalist countries is not severe in a relative sense, and improvements have been made. From an economic standpoint, the best policy for reducing poverty over time is economic growth. More important, capitalism is not the cause of poverty. The American economy has provided, through social programs and private giving resulting from economic growth, ample funds for reducing poverty significantly, if not entirely. The specific allocation of such public or private funds should not be blamed on free enterprise or the profit system.

Corporate pretax profits in the United States were $284 billion in 1986 (Table I), or less than one-half the total outlays devoted to social welfare expenditures. After-tax corporate profits in 1986 were $127 billion. Free benefits for those with a demonstrated need ($140 billion) plus private philanthropy ($87 billion) amount to almost twice as much as total after-tax corporate profits. Also, it should be remembered that only a portion of realized corporate profits is distributed in the form of dividends to the owners of businesses; the balance is retained for research and development, capital expenditures, and expansion, which creates additional employment and income.

An examination of empirical evidence suggests that capitalism is a superior perfomer in providing material needs.

This conclusion will satisfy some of those who hold misconceptions about the justice of capitalism resulting from a lack of information about the facts. But some are not persuaded, since poverty, inequality, and injustices still exist. The fact that less economic misery exists in free market economies than in command-type systems is a strong case for the justice of a profit-based economy. However, this is not the complete story, which leads to a philosophical discussion regarding alternative measures for judging economic justice.

Table I
Components of U.S. Gross National Product
and National Income, 1986
($ billions)

Gross National Product		$4,235.00
Personal Consumption Expenditures	$2,799.80	
Private Domestic Investment	671.00	
Net Exports	−105.50	
Government Purchases	869.70	
Minus Depreciation and Indirect Business Taxes		$−813.00
National Income		$3,422.00
Compensation of Employees	2,504.9	
Proprietors' Income	289.8	
Rental Income of Persons	16.7	
Corporate Profits	284.4	
Net Interest	326.2	

Note: Gross National Product (GNP) is the dollar sum of all final purchases. Intermediate-stage purchases are excluded to avoid double counting. National Income (NI) is a measure of the total cost of the final product and includes profits. The two measurements of economic activity are the same except for depreciation (which does not represent a current outlay) and indirect business taxes (which are merely collected by the business sector for the government).

Source: U.S. Bureau of the Census, *Statistical Abstract of the United States,* 108th ed. (Washington, D.C., 1987), p. 410.

Table II
Total and Per Capita Gross National Product
(Selected Countries)

COUNTRY	($ BILLIONS)	PER CAPITA IN 1983 CONSTANT DOLLARS		
		1975	1980	1984
India	$200.5	$215	$232	$258
Kenya	5.8	287	309	287
China	321.1	182	223	302
Sri Lanka	5.5	250	296	333
Indonesia	84.8	339	433	484
Turkey	54.3	962	977	1,061
Brazil	212.3	1,408	1,708	1,505
Portugal	19.6	1,635	1,975	1,894
Mexico	144.2	1,634	1,841	1,795
USSR	2,067.0	6,419	6,968	7,266
Hong Kong	30.7	——	——	6,230
Singapore	17.5	——	——	7,420
Japan	1,292.0	7,419	9,095	10,410
Sweden	95.3	10,240	10,650	11,050
United States	3,765.0	12,850	15,420	15,380

Source: U.S. Bureau of the Census, *Statistical Abstract of the United States,* 108th ed. (Washington, D.C., 1987), p. 805; and The World Bank, *World Development Report* (Washington, D.C.: Oxford University Press, 1987).

Table III
Measures of Well-being

COUNTRY	LIFE EXPECTANCY AT BIRTH	INFANT MORTALITY RATE UNDER AGE 1	POPULATION PER PHYSICIAN	ENROLLMENT IN HIGHER EDUCATION AS % OF AGE GROUP
India	56	89	3,700	9
Kenya	54	91	10,140	1
China	69	35	1.730	1
Sri Lanka	70	36	7,460	4
Indonesia	55	96	12,300	7
Turkey	64	84	1,530	9
Brazil	65	67	1,300	11
Portugal	74	19	500	12
Mexico	67	50	1,200	15
USSR	70	29	270	21
Hong Kong	76	9	1,300	13
Singapore	73	9	1,100	12
Japan	77	6	740	30
Sweden	77	6	410	38
United States	76	11	500	57

Note: Infant mortality rate is the number of infants who die before age 1 per thousand live births. The higher education enrollment is based on the 20–24 age group.

Source: The World Bank, *World Development Report* (Oxford University Press, 1987), and Paul Kennedy, *The Rise and Fall of the Great Powers* (New York: Random House, 1987).

Table IV
Consumer Statistics for Specific Items
(Selected Countries, 1985)

COUNTRY	PERSONS PER AUTOMOBILE	TELEPHONES PER 100 POPULATION	TELEVISIONS PER 1,000 POPULATION
India	525	0.5	5
Kenya	——	1.3	5
China	2,022	0.6	9
Sri Lanka	——	0.7	28
Indonesia	——	0.3	39
Turkey	51	6.7	148
Brazil	13	8.4	184
Portugal	——	18.0	157
Mexico	15	9.1	108
USSR	24	11.3	296
Hong Kong	——	42.4	236
Singapore	——	41.7	195
Japan	4.3	55.5	580
Sweden	——	89.0	390
United States	1.8	76.0	798

Source: U.S. Bureau of the Census, *Statistical Abstract of the United States,* 108th ed. (Washington, D.C., 1987), pp. 808–809.

Table V
Economic Activity and Poverty—United States

YEAR	# OF PERSONS BELOW POVERTY LEVEL (000)	POVERTY RATE %	POVERTY RATE WITH NONCASH BENEFITS %	GROWTH IN REAL GNP %	UNEMPLOYMENT RATE %
1959	33,490	22.4		6.0	5.5
1960	39,851	22.2		2.2	5.5
1961	39.628	21.9		2.6	6.7
1962	38,625	21.0		5.8	5.5
1963	36,436	19.5		4.0	5.7
1964	36,055	19.0		5.3	5.2
1965	33,185	17.3		6.0	4.5
1966	28,510	14.7		6.0	3.8
1967	27,769	14.2		2.7	3.8
1968	25,389	12.8		4.6	3.6
1969	24,147	12.1		2.8	3.5
1970	25,420	12.6		(0.2)*	4.9
1971	25,559	12.5		3.4	5.9
1972	24,460	11.9		5.7	5.6
1973	22,973	11.1		5.8	4.9
1974	23,370	11.2		(0.6)	5.6
1975	25,877	12.3		(1.2)	8.5
1976	24,975	11.8		5.4	7.7
1977	24,720	11.6		5.5	7.1
1978	24,497	11.4		5.0	6.1
1979	26,072	11.7		2.8	5.8
1980	29,272	13.0	8.1	(0.3)	7.1
1981	31,822	14.0	9.3	1.9	7.6
1982	34,398	15.0	10.3	(2.5)	9.7
1983	35,303	15.2	10.6	3.6	9.6
1984	33,700	14.4	9.8	6.8	7.5
1985	33,064	14.0	9.3	3.0	7.2
1986	32,370	13.6	9.0	2.9	7.0

Source: Poverty and poverty rate: *Poverty in the U.S., 1985* (U.S. Department of Commerce, Bureau of Census, October 1987). Change in GNP and unemployment rate: *Handbook of Cyclical Indicators, Supplement to Business Conditions Digest* (Washington, D.C.: U.S. Government Printing Office, 1987) and U.S. Bureau of the Census, *Statistical Abstract of the United States,* 108th ed. (Washington, D.C., 1987).

*Parentheses indicate a negative number.

61

Table VI
Median U.S. Family Income

YEAR	(1) TOTAL	(2) WHITE	(3) NONWHITE	(4) COLUMN 3 AS PERCENTAGE OF COLUMN 2
1960	$5,620	$5,835	$3,230	55.4%
1970	9,867	10,236	6,516	63.7%
1980	21,023	21,904	13,843	63.2%
1985	27,144	29,152	18,635	63.9%

Note: The numbers shown in this table are not adjusted for infaltion. By definition, median family income reflects the midpont of family incomes; one-half are above and one-half are below the median.

Source: *The 1988 Information Please Almanac* (Boston: Houghton Mifflin Company, 1988), pp. 51 and 54.

Table VII
Characteristics of the U.S. Poor—1986
(Percentage and Number of Persons below Poverty Level)

CATEGORY	PERCENTAGE BELOW POVERTY LEVEL	NUMBER BELOW POVERTY LEVEL
All persons	13.6%	32.4 million
White	11.0%	22.2 million
Black	31.1%	9.0 million
UNDER 16 YEARS OLD	21.0%	11.7 million
White	16.5%	6.4 million
Black	43.8%	3.7 million
PERSONS 65 AND OVER	12.4%	3.5 million
White	10.7%	2.7 million
Black	31.0%	0.7 million
REGION (ALL PERSONS):		
Northeast	10.5%	5.2 million
Midwest	13.0%	7.6 million
South	16.1%	13.1 million
West	13.2%	6.4 million
In families with		
Female head, no husband	34.6%	3.6 million

Note: Subcategories do not add up to 100% due to rounding off and omitted categories.

Source: U.S. Bureau of the Census, *Statistical Abstract of the United States,* 108th ed. (Washington, D.C., 1987), pp. 433–437.

Table VIII
Characteristics of the U.S. Poor—1986
(Percentage and Number of Families below Poverty Level)

CATEGORY	PERCENTAGE BELOW POVERTY LEVEL	NUMBER BELOW POVERTY LEVEL
All families	10.9%	7.0 million
White	8.6%	4.8 million
Black	28.0%	2.0 million
HOUSEHOLDER UNDER		
AGE 24	31.5%	0.9 million
White	26.3%	0.6 million
Black	58.6%	0.3 million
SIZE OF FAMILY		
2 persons	8.9%	2.4 million
7 persons or more	31.9%	0.4 million
EDUCATION		
Less than 8 years	25.5%	1.1 million
High school	9.5%	2.1 million
College, 1 year or more	4.0%	1.0 million

Note: Subcategories do not add up to 100% due to rounding off and omitted categories.

Source: U.S. Bureau of the Census, *Statistical Abstract of the United States,* 108th ed. (Washington, D.C., 1987), pp. 433–437.

Table IX
Poverty in the United States—1986

CATEGORY	EXCLUDING NONCASH BENEFITS		INCLUDING NONCASH BENEFITS	
	NUMBER (MILLIONS)	PERCENT BELOW POVERTY LEVEL	NUMBER (MILLIONS)	PERCENT BELOW POVERTY LEVEL
All persons	32.4	13.6%	21.4	9.0%
White	22.22	11.0%	14.9	7.4%
Black	9.0	31.1%	5.7	19.8%
Northeast	5.2	10.5%	2.7	5.4%
Midwest	7.6	13.0%	4.9	8.3%
South	13.1	16.1%	9.3	11.3%
West	6.4	13.2%	4.5	9.3%

Note: Noncash benefits include estimated market value of food, housing, and medical benefits.

Source: U.S. Bureau of the Census, *Statistical Abstract of the United States,* 108th ed. (Washington, D.C., 1987), p. 437.

Table X
The Poverty Gap—United States

1985 poverty level of Income, family of 4	$10,989
1985 estimated approximate earnings of poverty family	$5,000
Estimated family income shortfall	$5,989
Poverty gap—families below poverty level (7,223,000) times shortfall ($ billions)	$43.3
Poverty gap as percentage of Gross National Product	1.1%
Estimated families below poverty level including noncash benefits	5,350,000
Poverty gap ($ billions)	32.0
Alternative poverty gap as percentage of Gross National Product	0.8%

Source: Derived from the U.S. Bureau of the Census, *Statistical Abstract of the United States,* 108th ed. (Washington, D.C., 1987), pp. 433–437.

Table XI
Social Welfare Expenditures—United States

	1960	1985
Total federal and state ($ billions)	$52.3	$729.1
Total expenditures as percentage of GNP	10.3%	18.5%
Total expenditures as percentage of government outlays	38.4%	52.9%

Note: Includes federal and state expenditures.

Source: U.S. Bureau of the Census, *Statistical Abstract of the United States,* 108th ed. (Washington, D.C., 1987), p. 336.

Table XII
Cash and Noncash Benefits—United States, 1985

Total Households below Poverty Level	11,995,000
Total Households Receiving Noncash Benefits:	14,466,000
Below Poverty Level 7,067,000	
Above Poverty Level 7,399,000	
Total Benefits Received by Persons with Limited Income ($ millions)	$140,424

Note: Benefits received by persons with limited income includes federal and state outlays. Programs cover cash and noncash benefits to persons who make no payment and render no service in return.

Source: U.S. Bureau of the Census, *Statistical Abstract of the United States,* 108th ed. (Washington, D.C., 1987), pp. 336–337.

Table XIII
Percentage Share of Household Income in Twelve Countries

COUNTRY	LOW EST 20%	SECOND QUINTILE	THIRD QUINTILE	FOURTH QUINTILE	HIGHEST 20%	HIGHEST 10%
India	7.0	9.2	13.9	20.5	49.4	33.6
Kenya	2.6	6.3	11.5	19.2	60.4	45.8
Sri Lanka	5.8	10.1	14.1	20.3	49.8	34.7
Indonesia	6.6	7.8	12.6	23.6	49.4	34.0
Turkey	3.5	8.0	12.5	19.5	56.5	40.7
Brazil	2.0	5.0	9.4	17.0	66.6	50.6
Portugal	5.2	10.0	14.4	21.3	49.1	33.4
Mexico	2.9	7.0	12.0	20.4	57.7	40.6
Hong Kong	5.4	10.8	15.2	21.6	47.0	31.3
Japan	8.7	13.2	17.5	23.1	37.5	22.4
Sweden	7.4	13.1	16.8	21.0	41.7	28.1
U.S.	5.3	11.9	17.9	25.0	39.9	23.3

Note: The data for this table refer to the distribution of total disposable household income accruing to percentile groups of households ranked by total household income. The distributions cover rural and urban areas and refer to different years between 1970 and 1985.

Source: The World Bank, *World Development Report* (Washington, D.C.: Oxford University Press, 1987), Table 26, pp. 252–53.

Table XIV
Change in Compensation and Profits

	COMPOUND ANNUAL RATE OF CHANGE	
TIME PERIOD	COMPENSATION	PROFITS
1950–60	6.6%	2.8%
1960–70	7.5%	3.4%
1970–80	10.2%	10.2%
1980–85	8.2%	8.9%
1950–85	8.1%	5.9%

Source: *The 1988 Information Please Almanac* (Boston: Houghton Mifflin Company, 1988), p. 61.

Table XV
Compensation of Employees and Corporate Profit—United States

	AS PERCENT OF NATIONAL INCOME	
YEAR	COMPENSATION	PROFITS
1950	64.1%	15.6%
1960	71.0%	12.0%
1965	69.8%	13.5%
1970	75.4%	8.7%
1975	76.6%	7.9%
1980	75.3%	8.6%
1984	73.1%	9.0%
1985	73.5%	8.7%
1986	73.2%	8.3%

Note: Compensation of employees is income accruing to employees for wages and salaries and supplements to wages and salaries. It includes salaries for corporate officers, commissions, tips, and bonuses.

Source: *The 1988 Information Please Almanac* (Boston: Houghton Mifflin Company, 1988), p. 61, and U.S. Bureau of the Census, *Statistical Abstract of the United States,* 108th ed. (Washington, D.C., 1987), p. 411.

Table XVI
Central Government Expenditures—1985
(Selected Countries)

COUNTRY	AS PERCENT OF GROSS NATIONAL PRODUCT	PERCENTAGE OF EXPENDITURES DEVOTED TO					ALL OTHER
		DEFENSE	EDUCATION	WELFARE	HEALTH	ECONOMIC	
India	16.7%	18.8%	1.9%	4.4%	2.4%	27.0%	45.5%
Kenya	26.6	12.9	19.8	0.6	6.7	24.8	35.2
Sri Lanka	32.6	2.6	6.4	11.1	3.6	10.2	66.1
Indonesia	20.2	12.9	11.3	1.4	2.5	37.9	34.0
Turkey	25.7	10.9	10.0	3.6	1.8	19.6	54.1
Brazil	21.1	4.0	3.2	32.7	7.6	14.5	38.0
Mexico	24.9	2.7	12.4	11.9	1.5	27.2	44.3
Singapore	26.3	20.1	20.2	6.5	6.2	15.0	32.0
Sweden	46.5	6.4	8.6	50.1	1.2	6.8	26.9
United States	24.5	24.9	1.8	31.6	11.3	8.3	22.1

Note: This table includes expenditures by the Central Government. It excludes expenditures by Local and/or State Governments. Expenditures for economic services comprise public spending for regulation, support, and more efficient operation of business and employment opportunities. Other expenditures include amounts that could not be allocated to other components and spending for general administration of government.

Source: The World Bank, *World Development Report* (Washington, D.C.: Oxford University Press, 1987), Table 23, pp 246–47.

Table XVII
Private Philanthropy Funds, 1986—United States
($ billions)

Total Funds Given:		$87.2
Individuals	$71.7	
Foundations	5.2	
Corporations	4.5	
Charitable bequests	5.8	
Allocation of Funds:		$87.2
Religion	$40.9	
Health	12.3	
Education	12.7	
Human services	9.1	
Arts, humanities	5.8	
Public/society benefit	2.4	
Other	4.0	

Source: U.S. Bureau of the Census, *Statistical Abstract of the United States,* 108th ed. (Washington, D.C., 1987), p. 359.

Chapter V

Some Philosophical Issues

. . . by any reasonable standard, and by comparison both with the past and with other societies in the present, America has not done badly at all by the standard of equality. But equality as a social reality, as an aggregate of empirical data, is not what the debate is finally all about, it seems.[1]

The debate about the morality and economic justice of capitalism goes beyond the experience of actual results. Capitalism is criticized for its failure to achieve a more ideal level of economic justice, despite the superior results actually realized in practice. Some critics of free enterprise argue that a profit system creates lower moral standards and tends to make persons more selfish.

While empirical arguments regarding capitalism emphasize practical results, philosophical arguments involve more idealistic considerations. Peter Berger states:

For many, though, such empirical exercises do not touch on the core of their concerns. It is essentially the difficulty of one who would defend a reality against a dream of perfection. Capitalism, by its very nature, is a sober, practical, prosaic affair.[2]

Although capitalism is far from perfect, the system is not without philosophical support. Capitalism should not be considered morally inferior relative to other practical economic systems just because it falls short of an idealistic goal that no system has ever achieved. The relevant philosophical consideration is whether or not capitalism supports or hinders the realization of a more economically just and moral society. All existing economic systems are morally imperfect. Opinions differ on the economic arrangement most suitable for enhancing morality and justice, not only as between existing systems but also compared to a more ideal system that might be achieved in the future.

Morality and Economic Justice

Morality and justice, although closely related, are not exactly the same. Morality is concerned with the "right" and "wrong" inward intentions affecting actual behavior and ultimate results. Economic justice is the component of morality concerned with persons actually receiving the basic rights to which they are entitled as human beings. Thus economic justice is a necessary but not a sufficient condition for claiming that a system is moral. The philosophical side of the profits and morality debate involves two issues: whether capitalism is an economically just system and to what extent the system encourages inferior personal moral standards.

Distributive Justice

Various schemes have been suggested as the basis upon which economic benefits might be distributed in the most just manner. Among the various considerations are: an equal sharing by all, sharing based on individual need, a division according to individual effort, distribution according to overall societal contribution, a sharing based on individual merit, and different combinations of these considerations. Generally, the discussion of economic justice is grouped into one of several categories, depending on the degree of emphasis placed on these suggested distributive mechanisms.

The Utilitarian Concept

Utilitarianism recognizes the constantly changing conditions in society, and measures economic justice by the net aggregate benefits (utility) achieved.

The expediency of utilitarianism might involve a combination of various distributive techniques for determining how benefits and burdens are to be allocated to increase total utility. Although some individuals or groups may be treated unfairly or unequally, the utilitarian concept of economic justice is concerned with the greatest level of net benefits in the aggregate. This is not to say that maximization of efficiency or total income is always the primary consideration; both positive and negative effects of greater efficiency must be considered in arriving at the desired net result that maximizes aggregate social utility.

The Modified Egalitarian Concept

John Rawls of Harvard advocates a quasi-egalitarian concept of economic justice.[3] Rawl's primary condition for economic justice is liberty—all should have the most extensive set of basic liberties compatible with equal liberty for all. The second part of Rawls's theory deals with results as reflected in the incomes, opportunities, and self-respect of all individuals, but does not require the equality of results represented by pure egalitarianism. Inequalities are permitted in the modified egalitarian concept if the results of such inequality benefit the least well off in society—the maximin principle—and if the inequalities are attached to positions open to all under the condition of fair equality of opportunity.

Rawls argues that equality is necessary for a system of economic justice, including material benefits and opportunities, unless it can be demonstrated that inequality produces a more desirable outcome for the least well off. In relaxing the standard of equality relating to the second part of the theory, Rawls apparently recognizes the practical importance of efficiency to the long-term benefits of the worst off in society. He believes that members of society will accept the importance of some inequality as an abstract and impersonal theory of economic justice if there is a fair equality of opportunity and the resulting inequality is subject to the maximin principle.

The maximin principle relies on some undefined social index of primary goods for measuring the benefits of the least advantaged. The principle does not apply to each and every transaction, but rather to the conditions against which the transaction takes place. In other words, inequalities that make a functional contribution to the worst off as a group are permitted.

In theory, Rawls claims that the social index yardstick can take into account differences in abilities, efficiency, and motivations. Thus an agreed-upon index can reflect factors such as freeloaders, rewards based on contribution, and long-term economic efficiency. The important factors in economic justice suggested by Rawls are the protection of personal liberty, reciprocity in establishing the rules to protect the noncontingent rights of all persons, and the relative level of benefits received by the least well off.

An obvious objection to the modified egalitarian view of economic justice is the interference that may be necessary to protect the least advantaged. While Rawls argues that interference is justified if the result is favorable for the worst off, libertarians claim that interference itself violates fundamental rights.

The Libertarian Concept

Justice according to the libertarian view is based primarily on negative personal liberty, or noninterference. Libertarians argue that the maximin principle of modified eqalitarianism interferes with personal liberty. Robert Nozick of Harvard, an advocate of libertarianism, argues that any interference beyond that required to prevent one person from interfering with another's basic rights, such as in the protection against theft, force, and fraud, is not justified.[4]

According to the libertarian view, inequality in results, per se, is not relevant to a concept of economic justice, unless the inequality represents holdings acquired unjustly. Any amount of inequality in results is just if persons are entitled to the holdings they possess, i.e., the holdings are acquired originally or through transfers that do not violate negative rights. If holdings are not acquired in a just manner, rectification is required. Therefore, libertarians recognize the need for coercion and interference when holdings have been acquired unjustly. It is clear that libertarianism implies much less interference than does the quasi-egalitarian view.

One of the key differences between libertarianism and modified egalitarianism concerns the justification of interference to influence end results. Libertarians believe that interference, except for rectification and to protect interference from others in very broad basic rights, is not justified regardless of the distribution of results. The modified egalitarian view holds that interference is always justified if it improves results for the least well off.

The Socialist Concept

Socialism, as a concept of economic justice, is based on the criteria of personal need and more equality in holdings to prevent some from attaining unacceptable power over others. State socialism is based on common ownership of property by the state, contrary to the other concepts reviewed above that endorse private property rights. The state controls production under strict socialism, and a just distribution is based on individual needs as determined by the state. Personal liberty and economic freedom are unimportant in the socialist framework of justice.

Socialism has been modified in many respects, as has capitalism. As previously noted, the modern versions of each contain many common features. Further modifications will no doubt continue to be made in reaction to actual results and the perception of economic justice of the system providing those results. Some observers see more justice in a modified version of state socialism where all property is owned in common by workers rather than the State. Others believe that modern capitalism is actually moving in this direction with the rapidly expanding reservoir of pension assets owned by workers.

Although personal liberty and economic freedom are of lesser importance in a socialist system, some of its supporters believe that a modified version of socialism is the only way in which all persons can enjoy equal effective liberty. This distinction reflects to a large extent the key difference noted earlier between libertarianism and modified egalitarianism. Economic freedom is an important element in this distinction.

Economic Freedom

Frederick Hayek argues that inequality is an essential characteristic of a free society.[5] Hayek uses the term "merit" to describe the attributes of conduct that make it deserving of praise, regardless of the results realized by those who are actually benefited. "Value," on the other hand, is used by Hayek to describe the benefits as determined by those actually receiving them. Thus the advantage derived from an activity may be judged either by the value it provides the ultimate benefactor or by the praise that some other person bestows on it.

Generally speaking, it is the potential of the reward as revealed in the success of the value actually delivered to the end user that provides incentives for more persons to risk the time and effort for undertakings on which they alone are free to decide, rather than activities encouraged by duty and praise from others of their moral character. To judge an activity based on the praise of others presupposes knowledge of the reasons why the activity was undertaken, as well as who should benefit from the result.

Hayek argues that reward based on result is consistent with a free society. He concludes:

> A society in which the position of the individuals was made to correspond to human ideas of moral merit would therefore be the exact opposite of a free society. It would be a society in which people were rewarded for duty performed instead of for success, in which every move of every individual was guided by what other people thought he ought to do, and in which the individual was thus relieved of the responsibility and the risk of decision. But, if nobody's knowledge is sufficient to guide all human action, there is also no human being who is competent to reward all efforts according to merit.[6]

Economic freedom and personal liberty are important components of distributive justice. On the opposite side of the argument is the question of effective economic freedom. The argument for economic freedom presented by Hayek is based largely on the benefits of efficiency and personal incentives. It must be recognized, however, that some persons may end up as victims of the process of efficiency and they may not enjoy the necessary level of benefits required for economic justice regardless of the level of overall efficiency achieved. An important consideration is the trade-off between overall efficiency and the effective economic freedom of the least advantaged.

The Social Trade-off

The concept of economic justice involves the pattern of distribution and sharing in a society. A widely held notion is that capitalism results in some persons having "too much" and that justice would be improved if such excess was transferred to those who have "too little." Libertarians argue that focusing on "too much" and "too little" is irrelevant so long as the existing distribution reflects holdings acquired in a manner that does not violate negative rights. The modified egalitarian view claims that "too much" by some represents an injustice if such holdings come about at the expense of the worst off. Socialism is an extreme view that holds that justice should be based more on need and that all property should be owned in common by the State or workers to assure the just satisfaction of those needs regardless of individual freedom. Since economic justice involves the equitable resolution of real conflicting interests, the social trade-off between efficiency and equality is important.

The essence of the free market is an outcome that increases the national wealth of society by relying on personal incentives and the profit motive. While actual capitalism recognizes the importance of social welfare obligations, it is important that such modifications not destroy the longer-term benefits of efficiency. The desire to achieve more equality is not as simple as redistributing total output available for a given time period as if the total will remain unchanged. The total will almost certainly be lower in future periods if incentives are reduced. Incentives are created by the rewards bestowed on those who deliver benefits as determined by the ultimate user.

The experience of capitalism has been that by permitting economic freedom and incentives, a greater level of total national income is achieved without increasing the inequality of income, compared to planned economies, which destroy incentives by directly controlling distributive results. The modified egalitarian concept of Rawls holds that more equality for the disadvantaged is desirable, even if the result is a decrease in total national income. Modified egalitarianism, however, is not inconsistent with most any level of inequality if equal opportunity is available and the resulting benefits for the least advantaged are positive. In other words, the modified egalitarian solution permits wide tolerances for market efficiency. The libertarian view of maximum personal liberty argues for a minimum of constraints as the means of realizing the end objective of an overall increased level of well-being.

The efficiency and equality trade-off in practice describes the economic justice of a society. The important point in the trade-off is that the total benefits to be distributed are affected by incentives and desires of individuals. The fallacy of the socialist argument for more equality is the assumption that total income will remain unchanged by redistribution attempts and that personal liberty is unimportant. Utilitarianism, modified egalitarianism, and libertarianism each recognize the importance of the trade-off, but differ on the balance between efficiency and equality. Economic justice, it would appear, depends on the mix between efficiency and the rights of all individuals to enjoy certain basic economic benefits, but not necessarily equal results. Equality of results is not a requirement of economic justice.

Actual capitalism fits within the philosophical framework of various concepts of economic justice. To varying degrees, both critics and supporters of free enterprise recognize the importance of personal liberty, efficiency, and welfare benefits. The debate about capitalism and economic justice reflects various opinions regarding the *relative* importance of these different components of justice, not the total rejection of any single component.

Greed and Self-interest

Another part of the philosophical side of the profits and morality debate concerns the influence of a market system on moral standards. This view focuses on the effect of the free market on behavioral intentions as reflected in greed and selfishness.

In the view of many people, greed and self-interest are inferior moral standards. Therefore, since self-interest and personal incentives are recognized as important characteristics of a market economy, the morality of capitalism faces an immediate challenge that extends beyond the consideration of economic justice. While some of the observations already reviewed cast doubt on this negative moral view of capitalism, it is helpful to look more carefully at the connection between morality, greed, and capitalism. Is greed morally bad? Does capitalism encourage greed?

Although greed is generally viewed more negatively than self-interest from a moral perspective, it could be argued that the two merely reflect degrees of inferior moral behavior. Philosophical theories differ over the moral acceptability of self-interest; most, however, seem to support the acceptance of self-interest as a valid moral principle. Thus unless self-interest is rejected outright as morally unacceptable, then it must be said that the role of self-interest and personal incentives in a free market framework has moral support.

Drawing a clear dividing line between self-interest and greed is impossible. However, it is assumed for present purposes that a dividing line does exist, beyond which behavior takes on the character of greed and may be morally unacceptable. Some, no doubt, will strongly disagree with this assumption; if greed produces more overall benefits, it might justify negative moral behavior. While this view has practical appeal, it is a weak and unnecessary philosophical position for the support of capitalism. Greed may be consistent with most views of economic justice, including the quasi-egalitarian concept of Rawls, and still not meet the standard of moral acceptability.

Accepting for the moment that greed represents a moral character flaw, where does this leave us with respect to capitalism? It must be assumed that greed exists in all economic systems. Those economic systems that pay lip service to egalitarian policies fail to escape the greedy methods of their own elite, even while the masses suffer. However, greed in one system does not make it morally proper in another.

If greed is considered morally improper, the ultimate question is whether one system encourages more greed than another. Many who view capitalism as morally distasteful argue that a market economy encourages greed in more people. It is the extravagance and increased personal well-being of a larger percentage of the population in capitalist societies that provides the ammunition for this view. What is

81

often overlooked is the fact, as earlier demonstrated, that increased national wealth ends up benefiting most all citizens in a market economy, although some benefit more than others. In other words, it is the very success of capitalism, the success that provides benefits to more people, that leads to the narrow view that capitalism encourages greed. The strength or weakness of this argument reverts to one's view about the economic justice of capitalism.

If there was some acceptable measure, one could test the proposition of whether or not capitalism tends to encourage more greed. Suppose differences in the standard of living—income, GNP per capita, etc.—were used as a proxy measure; while the conclusion might be that some groups must surely be very greedy compared to others, another conclusion is that most all groups, in the United States for example, are greedy relative to most other countries. Using actual inequality as a measure fails to support the view that American capitalism promotes more greed, since as we have seen, inequality and poverty are no less apparent in noncapitalist countries.

There is increasing evidence that the material success in the United States is not leading to more greed, but to more caring and benevolence. Consider the following from the January 28, 1989, issue of the *Economist:*

> Americans give a far bigger proportion of their incomes to charity, and volunteer more of their time, than do people any where else.
>
> Generosity has increased in recent years. In 1987, people gave $76.5 billion to charity, or 2% of their income, up from 1.8% in 1981. Three-quarters of all families give an average of $790 a year. The poor give a bigger proportion of their incomes than the rich, and surprisingly, both poor and rich are more generous than people in the middle.[7]

Increasingly, American corporations are devoting more man hours and money to community projects for assisting those in need.

Michael Novak, writing in *Forbes Magazine* (November 27, 1989), says:

> In this country, the great unfolding theme is the turn from politics and economics to morals. A major change in the nation's ethics is underway. UCLA Professor James Wilson has described it as the surprising reappearance in intellectual and public discourse of the idea of character.[8]

Whether the above observations represent a significant change in moral character on the whole or merely isolated examples of special interest moral concerns is not known. Some philosophical theories hold that most all social action is ultimately based on motivations of self-interest in order to assure continuing social harmony. In accordance with this viewpoint, examples such as the above might reflect behavior based on self-interest. At least, capitalism does not destroy the prudence of moral behavior in a macro sense.

The prudence of moral action in the aggregate may not apply on a individual level. The interest of an individual may be best served by acting in an immoral fashion, although a strong argument can also be made for the prudence of personal moral behavior. It would appear that the criticism of capitalism based on the belief that the system encourages more greed falls into the category of individual behavior. However, the behavior of individuals is constrained to some extent by the prudent necessity of moral action in the aggregate.

More important, there seems to be more to moral behavior than a consideration of prudence alone. Most individuals seem to possess an inward desire of caring and compassion separate and apart from the necessity of moral behavior just to achieve social harmony or their own long-run selfish desires.

Rober Nozick, the champion of libertarianism, has recently modified his position. He now believes that the common interest in the well-being of all persons should be part of society's social policy. In *The Examined Life,* Nozick states:

> The libertarian position I once propounded now seems to me seriously inadequate, in part because it did not fully knit the humane considerations and joint cooperative activities it left room for more closely into its fabric.
>
> There are many sides of ourselves that seek self-expression, and even if the personal side were to be given priority, there is no reason to grant it sole sway. If symbolically expressing something is a way of intensifying its reality, we will not want to truncate the political realm so as to truncate the reality of our social solidarity and humane concern for others. I do not mean to imply that the public realm is only a matter of joint self-expression; we wish also by this actually to accomplish something and make things different, and we would not find some policies adequately expressive of solidarity with others if we believed they would not serve to help or sustain them.[9]

The humane consideration and caring for others helps to establish an important moral standard for society. The consideration, it appears, begins with the individual's real concern for others and not with the forethought of merely achieving social harmony.

Just because capitalism recognizes the importance of self-interest as a means of improving well-being does not mean that the system destroys existing moral standards and creates an ethical character flaw. While self-interest and greed exist in every society, including capitalism, there in no available evidence that capitalist societies encourage more greed. It would appear that capitalism encourages as much compassion, kindness, and generosity as do noncapitalist societies, if not more.

The success of capitalism has resulted in more persons achieving a status that increases their ability to be generous. In the process, average well-being has increased. Regardless of one's view about the moral nature of self-interest and greed, the free market does provide benefits to more people. Without free market conditions, the outcome would be lower benefits, with no indication that moral standards would be improved.

Socialism, utilitarianism, egalitarianism, and libertarianism each represent different views about economic justice. Except for socialism, each is consistent, in varying degrees, with modern capitalism. Socialism does not overcome the motivation of self-interest and greed, although it purports to enhance moral standards by deemphasizing self-interest.

Utilitarianism measures economic justice by the overall net social benefit. Self-interest is either acceptable or unacceptable depending on its effect on net social results. Libertarianism endorses self-interest and personal liberty as the key elements of economic justice above all other conditions. Egalitarianism, on the other hand, imposes restraints on personal liberty and self-interest for the benefit of the worse off in society. However, once the parameters are established, self-interest is clearly acceptable in the modified egalitarianism view of Rawls.

Except for those favoring the prospects of theoretical socialism as their preferred notion of morality, self-interest cannot be totally rejected as an element in the economic justice and morality equation. The real issue is one of balancing the consideration of self-interest, and the positive benefits so created, against some measure of the needs of all persons.

Arguments in support of self-interest do not prove the case

for the moral superiority of capitalism; moral standards of behavior cannot be proved or disproved. Likewise, self-interest and greed, which exist in all societies, do not prove the moral case against capitalism.

Self-interest is consistent with each of the modern versions of economic justice. Thus it is not the absence of self-interest that defines a just economic system. The relevant consideration for economic justice is balancing the positive effects of self-interest with the protection of the fundamental rights of all persons. Determining that mix seems to be what economic justice is about.

The moral nature of greed is a broader question relating to personal intentions and motivations that goes beyond economic justice. There is no evidence that more greed actually exists under capitalism. The usual argument that capitalism encourages more greed because the system endorses self-interest and personal incentives is an unsupported proposition. It is an unfair indictment of capitalism to jump from the recognized importance of self-interest to the proposition that the system causes more greed.

Chapter VI

The Bottom Line

Free will implies choice: the moral function of society, the way in which it best serves the moral needs of the individuals who compose it, is when it facilitates the process of choice, permits consciences to inform themselves, and so offers the individual the greatest possible opportunity to fulfill his part in the divine contract. That, essentially, is the moral basis of capitalism.[1]

The most significant moral criticisms of capitalism are the notions that the distribution of economic benefits is too unequal and that the system encourages greed. This chapter will attempt to pull together the various arguments in the economic justice and morality debate.

A Concept of Economic Justice

Economic justice is the connecting link between personal moral standards and the ethical nature of an economic system. Benefits and burdens have never been shared equally in any society. While opinions differ over how benefits should be distributed, the considerations generally include some combination of the following:

- individual personal liberty
- equality of results
- economic efficiency
- assistance for the least advantaged in society

Personal liberty can be divided into a negative and a positive component. *Negative liberty* refers to noninterference from others in the pursuit of self-determined interests. However, since some interference is always necessary to maintain social order, this right in a practical sense must be qualified to mean the right to equal noninterference. Interference, whatever the degree, implies some violation of negative liberty.

Positive liberty involves the ability, including the economic means, for individuals to satisfy their interests and needs. Negative liberty offers the opportunity to pursue self-determined interest, while positive liberty is concerned with the realization of actual results. An individual may enjoy the equal opportunity of becoming a physician (negative liberty), but may not possess the financial capability to succeed (positive liberty). Thus the realization of desired results does not always follow the opportunity to participate equally in the process.

Equal negative liberty is an important part of economic justice, but it is an insufficient condition.

Most disagreements about economic justice center around the degree of positive liberty necessary to achieve a just distribution of results without too much violation of negative liberty. In the extreme case, interference could go as far as guaranteeing complete equality of economic benefits. Complete equality of benefits, however, is inconsistent with noninterference and free choice. While equality of opportunity is part of economic justice, achieving more equality in actual results may violate the right to negative liberty, since people achieve at different levels. Satisfying both negative and positive liberty at the same time is difficult.

Altering the outcome resulting from an emphasis on the right of negative liberty affects personal incentives, which serve an important function in promoting economic growth and efficiency. It is not possible to have equal results and, at the same time, enjoy the favorable effects of efficiency. If positive liberty is pushed too far in order to achieve more equal results, the cost will be lower efficiency and less benefits for society in general. On the other hand, if positive liberty is ignored, suffering by some will always be severe.

There is little disagreement that some inequality is desirable for achieving economic efficiency. Arguments about the importance of positive liberty in the different concepts of economic justice reviewed earlier are about relative benefits, not about complete equality.

Positive liberty is part of the trade-off consideration between economic efficiency and assistance for the least advantaged. In other words, positive liberty is a consideration of the justice involved in altering results from the outcome that would occur with less interference. Thus the trade-off between economic efficiency and welfare must be considered when determining the degree of positive liberty required for economic justice.

Evidence over a long period of time for different countries indicates that economic growth produces favorable results for the poor and disadvantaged as a group. The incidence of poverty and the inequality of income improve with economic growth. Slower growth, or negative growth, tends to be harmful to those most in need of assistance. Nothing more than equal opportunity to participate in the process of increased growth offers the best chance for many of the least advantaged to improve their own status. However, while the level of economic growth may influence the size of the least advantaged group, it never eliminates the personal needs of some, especially in the short run.

Mobility up the economic ladder is experienced by many of the disadvantaged during periods of economic growth. It seems obvious that economic efficiency should not be ignored when considering economic justice; efficiency offers increased participation in the process and the outcome. A reduction in opportunity for those capable of gaining from economic growth and efficiency, including segments of the least advantaged group, must be taken into account in policies designed to assist special groups who are incapable of benefiting from efficiency.

Efficiency and growth alone, however, are insufficient for realizing a just distribution. The conditions associated with the process of efficiency and growth are based largely on the market process of personal incentives and rewards. Thus efficient growth by itself produces distributive results that tend to emphasize contribution in the aggregate rather than personalized needs. The impact of growth is uneven; all individuals do not share equally in economic results, regardless of their needs or the amount of growth actually experienced. Although efficiency benefits some of the least advantaged, others may be so permanently disadvantaged that economic growth alone is ineffective for satisfying the basic needs required of economic justice.

Since the impact of efficiency is uneven, assistance for the truly least advantaged must be considered in any concept of economic justice. But pushing direct assistance too far may affect personal incentives and hinder efficiency, which can end up in the long run hurting the marginally and temporarily disadvantaged.

The libertarian view of economic justice emphasizes negative liberty and noninterference in the economic process. Libertarians claim that interference infringes on economic justice by restricting personal liberty and incentives. However, a proper mix between efficiency and assistance must be considered in determining a just distribution of results, for the reasons already mentioned.

While the modified egalitarian view of economic justice suggested by Rawls emphasizes the personal needs of the least advantaged, it also recognizes the importance of efficiency. Despite permitted inequalities for promoting efficiency, the formulation of the modified egalitarian model implies a highly equal distribution of results. The permitted initial inequalities eventually become actual and personal. Even if the resulting inequality follows exactly the predetermined and endorsed pattern, those actually finding themselves disadvantaged may be dissatisfied with that result.

We might imagine that the initial and impersonal formulation of the egalitarian model occurred at some earlier period. Inequalities were projected to provide positive results for the least advantaged. At some later date, the least advantaged may be better off than the average at the beginning of the experiment, or they may end up even more disadvantaged than at the beginning. Projected inequalities will not reflect the results eventually experienced and may not be satisfactory to those most affected. The measure of the positive results accruing to the least advantaged is an empirical test. But what is the reference point, and over what time period is the outcome measured? Expectations at any point in time reflect changing circumstances.

Circumstances that result in certain individuals ending up in the least advantaged group are always personal and unique. Regardless of the reasons, dissatisfactions and expectations of the disadvantaged reflect the current status of others even if the least advantaged have also benefited in absolute terms. Furthermore, the resulting inequalities affect those who were not a part of the original agreement. Taking the least advantaged group on the whole, the degree of proposed inequality that maximizes overall benefits for the group may actually be consistent with maximum efficiency. However, the group is not homogeneous, and some individuals always remain disadvantaged even if the total group benefits more than expected.

The modified egalitarian model seems to go in different directions. One direction is toward efficiency, since efficiency is projected to help the least advantaged in total. A more likely direction is toward a highly equal distribution of projected results for the reasons suggested above. Minimizing hardship and inequality in light of an unknown outcome (veil of ignorance) will most likely be the overriding consideration in the initial formulation of the model, since those who will end up disadvantaged are unknown when the permitted inequalities are projected. If, as suggested by the modified egalitarian concept, everyone has an equal probability of becoming part of the least advantaged, the degree of projected inequality allowed will more than likely be minimized.

A middle-of-the-road egalitarian view, or a formulation that provides for continuing modifications as the status of the least advantaged changes, comes full circle back to a realistic consideration of the trade-off between efficiency and assistance as circumstances change. The ultimate empirical test of the effect of the trade-off on economic justice, including an appropriate test for the modified egalitarian concept of justice, depends on a more precise definition of the least advantaged group and the factors that influence the well-being of that group at each period of time.

Economic Justice Requires Balance

The conditions for achieving economic justice require a careful evaluation of the circumstances. While the efficiency of a market economy contributes significantly to economic justice, assistance for particular individuals involuntarily or permanently disadvantaged is always necessary. The nature and degree of assistance depends, to some extent at least, on the reasons for the needed assistance. While special assistance is required, the benefits derived from efficiency must also be considered.

Socialism, as an alternative view of economic justice, fails to meet the conditions of justice outlined above. Ultimate communism pretends to offer a just solution by hypothetically removing the conflicts that create the reason for a consideration of economic justice in the first place. Existing socialism does not eliminate conflicts or satisfy basic needs as well as existing capitalism.

Existing capitalism is a mixture of conditions for encouraging efficiency and providing assistance to those unable or incapable of participation in the results. It recognizes the importance of both conditions of economic justice as it attempts to balance the right to negative liberty with the trade-off between conflicting claims and basic needs. One of the advantages of existing capitalism is that it has provided assistance to the worst off while encouraging personal incentives and efficiency. Social welfare expenditures, progressive taxation, and special-purpose tax policies reflect attempts to balance current and long-term aspects for the conditions of economic justice. The actual mix in existing capitalism is decided by economic, political, and moral checks and balances. If personal liberty, efficiency, and assistance for the least advantaged are not adequately balanced, economic justice suffers in any economic system, including capitalism.

The modified egalitarian view pushes toward a mixture of more positive liberty, while libertarianism emphasizes negative liberty. Actual capitalism is a compromise of sorts between these more extreme views, a compromise decided in a social environment permitting open debate and consensus. Modern capitalism falls along a continuum of opinions about economic justice. The relevant position on the continuum for achieving economic justice is one that takes into account the conditions of justice over a range of values that considers the effect of the trade-off between efficiency and welfare. Of course, opinions vary about the best mixture.

Maximizing economic justice at any point in time is compounded by the lack of a generally accepted measure for the dependent variable to be maximized. How is economic justice measured? Is the best measure the lowest possible unemployment rate? The least amount of inequality in the process or results? The most efficient system for growth? Or some other measure? Arguments about economic justice have as much to do with disagreements about the dependent variable as about the particular economic arrangement considered most conducive for realizing a just distribution. The system is merely the means of achieving the desired result once the measure is selected.

An economic system may be considered just or unjust depending on opinions about the dependent variable(s) selected for emphasis. Regardless of opinions about the measure selected, a framework for analyzing the mixture of efficiency and assistance for the least advantaged is necessary. The "Economic Justice Matrix" presents a framework for analyzing the mixture, assuming the negative liberty condition for economic justice is met at all times. The measure of economic justice may be one of the dependent variables suggested above or some other measure.

Economic Justice Matrix

The Least Advantaged	Time Frame	
	Short-term	Long-term
Permanent	I Greatest assistance	II Greatest assistance
Marginal	III Greatest assistance	IV Modest assistance
Temporary	V Modest assistance	VI Little or no assistance

Individuals are in the least advantaged group at any point in time for various reasons, and the makeup of the group is not constant. Some are permanently disadvantaged and no amount of economic efficiency can help their situation. Others are at the threshold of the least advantaged group, where a modest change in economic conditions can move them into a different category. Some others are only temporarily disadvantaged, and the assurance of negative liberty may be sufficient to improve their position without any direct assitance.

The entire least advantaged group, which is generally defined by reference to some minimum standard of material well-being, must be disaggregated. Those permanently disadvantaged may be children, senior citizens, and the physically and mentally disabled. The marginally worst off may be those who by education, ability, or training will always be relegated to borderline results. Those temporarily disadvantaged may be new entrants into the work force and those unemployed because of special factors but capable of improved results on their own in a growing economy.

Having classified the least advantaged group according to the reasons for their condition, the next consideration is the time frame. Efficiency is an important variable over the long run for assisting all groups. All those in the least advantaged group may require some assistance in the immediate short run. The nature and degree of assistance depend on the different reasons and their impact on the efficiency of the system. The permanently disadvantaged require the greatest amount of assistance in the long run as well as the short run, while the marginally and temporarily worst off may be helped most by a long-run emphasis on efficiency.

The degree of assistance required, based on some selected index of need, depends on the different reasons for the assistance and the time frame most appropriate. The degree of assistance is indicated in the six matrix cells in the "Economic Justice Matrix." In the short run, a high level of assistance should be directed to the permanently and marginally disadvantaged, while less assistance is necessary for the temporary category; in the long run, the need for assistance remains high for the permanently disadvantaged, while less assistance or none at all is needed for the other two groups. The level of assistance depends on the severity of the need, the impact of the assistance on efficiency, and the time frame.

The point of the matrix framework is that both efficiency and direct assistance must be considered. The trade-off depends on the different reasons for the least advantaged being part of that group. On balance, economic justice involves some mixture of efficiency and welfare, rather than all of one and none of the other. The makeup of the least advantaged group is not static; the group changes over time and is directly affected by mobility and increased opportunity created by efficiency and growth.

The view of economic justice presented above is consistent with the modified egalitarian model of Rawls. It also contains an essential element of utilitarianism, which views economic justice as the expedient maximization of the net social good. Utilitarianism, however, considers the fundamental needs of individuals only as a by-product of social efficiency. Libertarian considerations, although important over a range of the matrix solution outlined, provide an unacceptable solution for other parts of the matrix framework. None of the views is completely inconsistent with modern capitalism, however. The key difference is the impact of the trade-off between efficiency and assistance in meeting the needs of different categories of the least advantaged.

A particular formation of the modified egalitarian model is a situation that defines the least advantaged as those incapable of benefiting from the favorable results of efficiency and growth, i.e., the permanently worst off. This situation might be described by cells I, II, and III in the matrix diagram. Assistance for these subgroups, especially those falling in cells I and II, requires special attention and may not be helped by a libertarian emphasis. Those falling in cells IV, V, and VI may benefit more in the long run from a libertarian emphasis.

The framework presented here is merely an attempt to extend the theoretical formulation of the modified egalitarian view in a practical direction. Additional analysis is required in order to more precisely define a realistic and workable index for measuring economic justice. Once an appropriate measure is developed and a time frame is specified, the various trade-offs can be better understood and evaluated in light of the various concepts of economic justice. Until this is accomplished, arguments for and against the alternative views of economic justice will remain one-sided, depending on the trade-off implicit in the definition of economic justice underlying the particular viewpoint of those on different sides of the debate.

The various elements of economic justice reviewed above seem to support the case for modern capitalism to a greater extent than proving the case against it. In the final analysis, economic justice depends on a careful evaluation of the gains and losses in the practical trade-off between overall efficiency and welfare.

Moral Basis of Capitalism

Much of the criticism of capitalism stems from a concern that can also be directed to all other economic systems, i.e., inadequate benefits received by the disadvantaged and the influence of the system on personal moral standards. Morality looks to the inward desires and moral standards of individuals to freely assist others regardless of the circumstances. Economic justice seeks to impose some form of economic and social parameters to ensure the satisfaction of the basic needs of all persons. These parameters by necessity must be molded into the economic system.

Capitalism provides an efficient means of producing goods and services from which needs are satisfied. Efficiency is achieved, in part, from an emphasis on self-interest and personal incentives. Increased efficiency, however, need not eliminate or lower the moral standards of individuals; it certainly does not preclude high moral standards and behavior. At worst, the impact of efficiency on a particular society would appear to be morally neutral compared to the same individuals in a society organized in some alternative economic fashion. The profit system should be considered morally inferior only if efficiency contributes to a lowering of moral standards.

The main problem with showing moral purpose of any economic system is the fact that morality encompasses more than economic justice. Capitalism promises no more than material benefits, while ultimate socialism promises more but thus far in history has been incapable of satisfactory performance or an improvement in moral behavior. Morality depends on free choice in deciding between "right" and "wrong" behavior. Norman states:

> Morality requires self-interest to become enlightened; that is to say, the productive use of personal resources in the creation of wealth will itself suggest the context for the exercise of moral considerations in social relationships, rather than on predetermined blueprints of economic morality, enforced by the rule of law, fashioned by those who have arrived at what they think is best for everyone, and unvarying in its application in a world where men are enormously diverse in their moral sense and personal responsibility.[2]

It is only when a person freely decides between right and wrong behaviour that a sense of morality exists. If individual choice is taken away, morality loses much, if not all, meaning.
Professor Hayek states:

> It is an old discovery that morals and moral values will grow only in an environment of freedom, and that, in general, moral standards of people and classes are high only when they have long enjoyed freedom and proportional to the amount of freedom they have possessed. That freedom is the matrix required for the growth of moral values is almost self-evident. It is only where the individual has choice, and its inherent responsibility, that he has occasion to affirm existing values, to contribute to their further growth, and to earn moral merit.[3]

Once established, the freedom that contributes to the moral foundation of the system also works in harmony with other aspects of social cooperation to promote the material needs and economic justice of society. The same freedom that is necessary for moral development must allow the individual to utilize his talents and resources as he freely chooses. It is through the natural tendency for the free pursuit of self-interest that increased well-being is best developed. This freehold interest of the individual captures an instinct of human nature (self-interest) that promotes the general welfare of society. However, this same freedom of choice allows at any step along the way the opportunity for the individual to pursue any other aim he chooses.

As previously noted, economic justice alone is an insufficient condition for claiming any economic system is a moral one. To the extent that capitalism can be shown to encourage lower moral standards, the system will always be criticized from a moral point of view regardless of the level of justice provided by the system. There are varying opinions but no available evidence to support the view that capitalism actually encourages lower moral standards.

Conclusion

The profits and morality debate is not about the failure of capitalism and certainly not about the success of some alternative economic system such as socialism. This is abundantly clear based on a review of empirical evidence. Philosophical arguments are less obvious, more indirect, and subject to many opinions.

What the debate is really all about is a common concern for the welfare of the disadvantaged. Arguments about the moral nature of the profit system are only the "tip of the iceberg" in the long-standing debate about social justice and morality, which predates capitalism by many centuries. This is not to suggest that the current profits and morality debate should be dismissed as merely a passing fad. To the contrary, the debate is relevant because it is always current; economic justice and personal moral standards can always be improved. There seems to be a tendency by some to suddenly view profits and capitalism as the source of economic injustice and lower moral standards, a view that is now refuted.

Arguments on both sides of the issue are much too short-sighted. Those who support the profit system, believing their critics to be idealistic and unrealistic, too often turn a deaf ear to the arguments. Opponents, on the other hand, reject the profit system too quickly, maybe because it offers a convenient excuse for society's collective failure to achieve their particular idea of greater justice and morality. Progress toward social justice requires improved communications to overcome these semantic differences and misperceptions. Each side is guilty of quick conclusions.

The first barrier to overcome is recognizing the common ground. A commonality of interest, or so it appears, is the trait of human nature that produces a sincere concern for the disadvantaged. While reasonable people will, of course, disagree about appropriate means, each side in the debate advances their arguments as if the other side did not share this inherent trait of compassion. The critics of capitalism, if they are to mount an effective argument, must demonstrate that a free market economy in some way diminishes this desire of compassion.

F.A. Hayek, one of the strongest advocates of free enterprise, is careful to separate the importance of the efficiency of a market system from the purposes to which such efficiency is ultimately directed. Morality is derived ultimately from the personal attitudes and decisions of how the means are used and not from the system that produces those means. Hayek states:

> When we defend the free enterprise system we must always remember that we must not confuse efficiency in providing means with the purposes which they serve. A society which

has no other standard than efficiency will indeed waste that efficiency. If men are to be free to use their talents to provide us with the means we want, we must remunerate them in accordance with the values these means have to us. Nevertheless, we ought to esteem them only in accordance with the use they make of the means at their disposal.[4]

Capitalism provides an efficient means of organizing economic activity and producing material results. Economics and ethics are not contradictory, as some believe; to support capitalism is not unchristian, nor should support of the system be regarded as holding moral and ethical standards in lesser esteem than material benefits. Free choice and efficiency are important elements in providing material means to the largest number of people. The manner in which individuals decide how these benefits are to be used, including the influence of such decisions on moral behavior, is the ultimate measure of the morality of the system.

Evidence of the benefits derived from free enterprise is showing up in country after country. Although this does not prove the moral superiority of capitalism, it puts to rest some of the moral guilt feelings about the success of the system. The claim that free enterprise is morally inferior is a weak position to support in view of the growing evidence to the contrary. Pope John Paul II observes:

In today's world, among other rights, the right of economic initiative is often suppressed. Yet it is a right which is important not only for the individual but also for the common good. Experience shows us that the denial of this right, or its limitation in the name of an alleged equality of everyone in society, diminishes or in practice absolutely destroys the spirit of initiative, that is to say, the creative subjectivity of the citizen. As a consequence, there arises not so much a true equality as a leveling down.[5]

The benefits derived from "the right of economic initiative," "the spirit of initiative," and "the creative subjectivity of the citizen" sound strikingly similar to the "invisible hand" of Adam Smith.

Notes

Chapter I. The Profit System under Attack

1. Paul Johnson, "Has Capitalism a Future?" in *Will Capitalism Survive?* (Washington, D.C.: Ethics and Public Policy Center, 1979), p.6.
2. The Inter-Religious Task Force for Social Action, *Must We Choose Sides* (New York: Episcopal Church Publishing Company, 1979), p. 63.
3. Ibid.
4. Methodist Federation for Social Action, *A Critical Study of Capitalism and the Christian Faith* (New York: Shalom House, 1976), p. 1.
5. Christians For Socialism, U.S.A., *Where We Stand* (Detroit: CFS National Office, April 1982).
6. The Inter-Religious Task Force for Social Action, *Must We Choose Sides,* p. 63
7. Ernest W. Lefever, *Amsterdam to Nairobi: The World Council of Churches and The Third World* (Washington, D.C.: Ethics and Public Policy Center, 1979), p. 49.
8. Rael Jean Isaac and Erich Isaac, *Sanctifying Revolution, Mainline Churchmen Turn Radical* (Washington, D.C.: Ethics and Public Center, Report 31, May 1981), pp. 5 and 9.
9. Ibid., p. 9.
10. Ibid., p. 19.

Chapter II. Market and Planned Economies

1. Ludwig Von Mises, *The Anti-Capitalist Mentality* (South Holland,

Illinois: Libertarian Press, 1972), p.83.

2. F. A. Hayek, *Capitalism and the Historians* (Chicago: University of Chicago Press, 1954), p. 13.

3. Ibid., p. 21.

4. Ibid., p. 18.

5. Paul A. Samuelson and William D. Nordhaus, *Economics,* 12th ed. (New York: McGraw-Hill Book Company, 1985), p. 41.

6. Vincent Barry, *Moral Issues in Business,* 3d ed. (Belmont, California: Wadsworth Publishing Company, 1986), p. 86.

7. Adam Smith, *An Inquiry into the Nature and Causes of the Wealth of Nations* (New York: Modern Library, 1937), p. 423.

8. Ibid.

9. Samuelson and Nordhous, *Economics,* p. 663.

Chapter III. Reasons for the Conflict

1. Edward R. Norman, *The Denigration of Capitalism,* (Washington, D.C.: American Enterprise Institute for Public Policy Research, 1979), p. 20.

2. Warren T. Brookes, *The Economy in Mind* (New York: Universe Books, 1982), p. 209.

3. Ibid., p. 211.

4. Roger L. Shinn, "From Theology to Social Decisions—and Return," in *Morality of the Market and Economic Perspectives* (Vancouver, British Columbia: The Fraser Institute, 1982), p. 182.

5. Peter L. Berger, *The Capitalist Revolution* (New York: Basic Books, 1986), pp. 196–98.

6. Ibid., p. 199.

7. Peter F. Drucker, "What Is Business Ethics," in *Across the Board* (New York: The Conference Board, October 1981), p. 24.

8. Michael Novak, *The Spirit of Democratic Capitalism* (New York: Simon and Schuster, 1982), p. 213.

9. U.S. Bishops' Pastoral Message and Letter, *Economic Justice for All: Catholic Social Teaching and the U.S. Economy,* November 1986.

10. Ibid., section 16.

11. Ibid., section 19.
12. Paul A. Samuelson, and William D. Nordhaus, *Economics,* 12th ed. (New York: McGraw-Hill Book Company, 1985), p. 750.

Chapter IV. The Historical Results of Capitalism

1. Peter L. Berger, *The Capitalist Revolution* (New York: Basic Books, 1986), p. 37.
2. Paul Johnson, *Will Capitalism Survive* (Washington, D.C.: Ethics and Public Policy Center, 1979), p. 5.
3. Peter L. Berger, *Capitalism and Equality in America,* vol. 1 (New York: Hamilton Press, 1987), p. 4.
4. Ibid.
5. Berger, *The Capitalist Revolution,* p. 153.
6. Ibid., p. 176.
7. Paul A. Samuelson, and William D. Nordhaus, *Economics,* 12th ed. (New York: McGraw-Hill Book Company, 1985), p. 776.
8. *The Commercial Appeal,* March 29, 1988 (Memphis, Tennessee: Joseph R. Williams). Reprinted by permission of *The Commercial Appeal.*
9. Nicholas Eberstadt, "Progress against Poverty in Communist and Non-Communist Countries in the Postwar Era," in Peter Berger, ed., *Modern Capitalism,* vol. 2 (New York: Hamilton Press, 1987), p. 77.
10. Samuelson and Nordhaus, *Economics,* p. 748.
11. Ibid., p. 777.
12. Berger, *The Capitalist Revolution,* p. 183.
13. Esther Fein, the New York Times News Service, reported in the *Commercial Appeal* (Memphis, Tennessee), January 29, 1989. Reprinted by permission of *The Commercial Appeal.*
14. Rebecca Blank, *Desegregating the Effect of the Business Cycle on the Distribution of Income,* National Bureau of Economics Research, Working Paper Number 2397, Princeton, 1987, p. 2.
15. Walter D. Connor, "Social Mobility and Democratic Capitalism in America," in Peter Berger, ed., *Modern Capitalism,* vol. 1

(New York: Hamilton Press, 1988), p. 8.

16. Michael Novak, *Freedom with Justice* (San Francisco: Harper and Row Publishers, 1984), p. 43.
17. Gustav F. Papanek, "Capitalist Developments and Income Distribution," in Berger, *Modern Capitalism,* vol. 2.
18. Ibid.
19. Friedrick A. Hayek, *The Constitution of Liberty* (Chicago: University of Chicago Press, 1960), p. 45.
20. U.S. Bureau of the Census, *Statistical Abstract of the United States,* 108th ed. (Washington, D.C., 1987), pp. 485 and 517.
21. "Americans Give," *Economist* (London), January 28–February 3, 1989, p. 22.

Chapter V. Some Philosophical Issues

1. Peter L. Berger, *Capitalism and Equality in America,* vol. 1 (New York: Hamilton Press, 1987), p. 11.
2. Ibid., p. 13.
3. John Rawls, "A Contractarian Theory of Justice," in Tom Beauchamp and Terry Pinkard, eds., *Ethics and Public Policy,* 2d ed. (Englewood Cliffs, New Jersey: Prentice-Hall, 1983), p. 157.
4. Robert Nozick, "A Libertarian Theory of Justice," in Beauchamp and Pinkard, *Ethics and Public Policy,* p. 159.
5. Friederich A. Hayek, *The Constitution of Liberty* (Chicago: University of Chicago Press, 1960), p. 94.
6. Ibid., p. 97.
7. "Americans Give," *Economist* (London), January 28–February 3, 1989, p. 22.
8. Michael Novak, "Good-bye to Materialism," *Forbes Magazine* (New York), November 27, 1989.
9. Robert Nozick, *The Examined Life* (New York: Simon and Schuster, 1989), pp. 286–87.

Chapter VI. The Bottom Line

1. Paul Johnson, "Is There a Moral Basis for Capitalism?," *Value Line,* July 18, 1980, p. 533.
2. Edward R. Norman, *Denigration of Capitalism,* edited by Michael Novak (Washington, D.C.: American Enterprise Institute for Public Policy Research, 1979), p. 9.
3. F. A. Hayek, *The Foundations of Morality,* edited by Henry Hazlitt (Los Angeles: Nash Publishing, 1964), p. 236.
4. F. A. Hayek, *Studies in Philosophy, Politics and Economics* (New York: Simon and Schuster, 1967), p. 322.
5. Michael Novak, "The Pope of Enterprise," *Forbes Magazine* (New York), June 26, 1989, p. 70.